'Read it and be wise.'

From the Foreword by Lieutenant General David Morrison AO, Australian of the Year 2016

'Australia's tradition of military leadership has a lot to offer leaders in business, from sensible structures and disciplines to the clear obligation to care for one's people. Nick Jans conveys that leadership tradition with great clarity.'

Paul Franklin, General Manager Payments, National Australia Bank

'This book provides great insights into leadership that can be applied to everyday corporations and not just within the military, so that we as readers can make better leaders within our differing environments.'

Linda Rudd MRICS, Senior Director, Asset Management Services, Knight Frank Australia Pty Ltd

'War is difficult, highly complex and unpredictable, and success on the battlefield requires strong consistent leadership and systems across various functions. Nicholas Jans draws out those skills, knowledge and attributes for business leaders to apply within their organisation and marketplace.'

David John Sloan BCom, EMBA, GAICD, General Manager/Owner, Bulla Dairy Foods (Ex-Reserve soldier, 4/19 PWLH, Australian Army)

'The mention of "military leadership" can invoke images of blinding heroics, risking a flawed start to any study into leadership. Nick Jans simply asks that we start with the military's values, inviting us to follow evidence of why the military leads as it does, allowing us to determine what lessons can be drawn out.'

John Keith, Chairman, Atomo Diagnostics

LEADERSHIP SECRETS
of the
AUSTRALIAN ARMY

Royalties from sales of *Leadership Secrets of the Australian Army* are going to Soldier On, a support services provider for veterans of the military, emergency services and national security agencies.

LEADERSHIP SECRETS
of the
AUSTRALIAN ARMY

Learn from the best and inspire your team for great results

Brigadier Nicholas Jans (Ret'd), OAM

ALLEN&UNWIN
SYDNEY • MELBOURNE • AUCKLAND • LONDON

First published in 2018

Allen & Unwin
83 Alexander Street
Crows Nest NSW 2065
Australia
Phone: (61 2) 8425 0100
Email: info@allenandunwin.com
Web: www.allenandunwin.com

A catalogue record for this book is available from the National Library of Australia

ISBN 978 1 76063 180 2

Internal design by Midland Typesetters, Australia
Set in 11.5/17.5 pt Minion Pro by Midland Typesetters, Australia
Printed and bound in Australia by Pegasus Media & Logistics

10 9 8

To Colonel Michael Crawford, MBE, who died on 22 July 2015, respected and remembered by many, not least of whom are his former subordinates Nick Jans and Noel Turnbull.

A culture of adaptability is vital to survival in the armed services. As business executives cope with increasing unpredictability, they can take a page from the military's book.

Harvard Business Review, November 2010

Contents

List of tables		xi
Foreword		xiii
Prologue		xv
1	Leadership we can believe in	1
2	Leadership, culture and context	13
3	Looking at leadership	27
4	The military leadership ethos	41
5	The 3Rs of leadership: An overview	57
6	Representing: The role model	69
7	Relating: The supportive people manager	87
8	Running the team: The engaging catalyst	103
9	Building an organisation by building its people	119
10	It's the backswing, stupid	135

Appendix 1: Contemporary Army structure   145

Appendix 2: Making the leader-as-catalyst approach work 149

Glossary   155

Acknowledgements   159

Notes   161

Index   185

List of tables

5.1   Building followership by practising the 3Rs of leadership   60

6.1   Building followership by Representing what the group
stands for   71

7.1   Building followership by Relating constructively with
group members   91

8.1   Building followership by Running the team in ways
that engage group members   106

8.2   The AAR   115

A1.1   Officers (commissioned)   147

A1.2   Other ranks (soldiers, sailors, airmen/airwomen)   147

Notes   The 3Rs model compared to two mainstream and
widely-used leadership models   177

Foreword

A long time ago, when I was a junior officer in the great national institution that is our Army, I was struggling to find my place, not just in my newfound profession but also in life more generally. It was 1982 and I was an instructor at the School of Infantry, at Singleton in the Hunter Valley in New South Wales.

I had joined the Army without anything approaching a vocation. To be honest, I had finished an indifferent Arts degree at the Australian National University, I was broke and I didn't want to stay in Canberra. I thought I would 'do' several years and then move on to something different, and it was working out that way until one particular event that gave me much needed ballast in my life.

I had let the team down. My memories are hazy as to the actual circumstances but I knew that I had performed to a less than ideal benchmark. I cared, but at one level I didn't. I was ready to leave. I was a lieutenant, and the sergeant working for me was clearly disappointed in my commitment. He was so much my senior in terms of life and military experience and he said, without any obvious signs of deference, 'I want a word with you.' I was ushered into the office we shared and he closed the door. He looked directly at me and said, 'You need to realise that you are the legacy of all who have served before you—thousands of men and women who put service before self. You are the legacy of your parents, your teachers and your friends. What you are not asking yourself is about the legacy you are going to leave.'

It's all about legacy. That is the gift we all get to give. It can be big, sometimes touching nations and huge corporate entities if that is the station in life we attain, or it can be small but vital, touching families and friends if we live a life more private. But big or small, legacy is delivered through leadership and belief.

And that is the focus of this book—leadership that continues to resonate and have relevance, even after we have left the roles in which we were required to lead.

Nick Jans has practical experience to draw on, but it is the insights of those who have shared their stories that really speak to what authentic leadership is all about. No one is born a natural leader. We all need to think deeply about the attributes required to exercise effective leadership, to find role models from whom we take inspiration, and to learn the deeply human skills that will enable us to leave that legacy. *Leadership Secrets of the Australian Army* has all this 'in spades'. Read it and be wise.

Lieutenant General David Morrison, AO
Former Chief of Army and 2016 Australian of the Year

Prologue

The seeds from which this book grew were planted in the first week of February 2009. On the Thursday I ran a seminar on Army leadership as part of a new Executive MBA at Sydney University. Buoyed by its reception, I travelled home on the Saturday morning, 7 February, to the little town of Marysville in Victoria's Central Highlands with ideas for a book running through my mind.

I arrived just in time to help my wife defend our house against the worst bushfire ever recorded in Australia. Across Victoria on that Black Saturday, 173 people died and more than 2000 houses were destroyed. All plans were thrust into the background as Judy and I joined a small community leadership group working on local recovery.

My experiences in community leadership during the following year confirmed many of the principles I had highlighted in my Sydney University seminar. And as I drew instinctively on habits embedded by 25 years in uniform, supplemented by my study of leadership in the previous decade, I saw their applicability over and over again.

I developed a simple model that shows how the various core activities of leadership fit together, the model that became the '3Rs of leadership' described in this book.

It was my guide for day-to-day and often moment-to-moment action, and for reflecting on and learning from my performance. For the first time in my experience as a leader I was able to see clearly what I should be doing, and to see why certain things were working and others weren't. Similarly, I used the model to analyse the behaviour of the many outstanding leaders who visited us and thus get a better idea of just what underpinned their 'magic'.

For example, I relearned the importance of effective communication: of its effect on group confidence, and the trust that flowed to someone who could calmly and coherently explain an issue and the preferred option for dealing with it. It brought home again and again the importance of using the communication process to influence as well as to inform, and of consulting people not just to solicit their views but also to show them that those views are valued.

All this was not without its many gaffes. In fact, communication figured in one of the more embarrassing examples. It occurred in late March during the Annual General Meeting of the Marysville Community Golf & Bowls Club. I had just been elected as its president, and in my acceptance speech I spoke of how we would pull ourselves together and come back stronger than ever—not just for the benefit of the club but also for the benefit of the community as a whole, as it was the only viable business of any size left in the village. But I overstepped the mark when I ended on a somewhat pompous note by speaking of the deep satisfaction of 'doing something bigger than ourselves'.

After the meeting I was approached by a somewhat irritated member, who pointed out to me that, his house having been destroyed in the bushfire, he was putting all his energies into family recovery, thank you very much, and had very little left that could be diverted 'to a higher cause', however worthy. Whoops! It was too late to grab everybody's attention again and tone down what I'd said, so instead I mingled with the members as they sipped cups of tea before heading home, quietly asking each small group for their reactions to the proposed strategy of helping to 'get us back on our feet'. Put in this way—in a more down-to-earth and 'Australian' way—my expression of this vision was much more palatable.

I continued with the process of applying, reflecting and learning, confirming again and again the dictum that leadership is an area in which one should never—can never—stop learning.

Meanwhile, I never let go of my dream of communicating all this to a wider audience. Every subsequent February I ran a seminar at Sydney University, and the positive way each one was received simply reinforced this dream. And when, a few years down the track, I encountered a former comrade—Vietnam-era national serviceman, successful businessman and communications expert, Noel Turnbull—who volunteered to help me in the project, I found a way to make it possible.

Noel was invaluable in so many ways. He helped me to find the right 'voice' and he also gained access to, and helped to interview, other former national service officers who had served in the 1960s and '70s. Their reflections became a key part of the large database of experiences from which Noel and I drew insights and illustrations.

Noel joins me in the hope that this book will help you to develop a more self-aware, engaging and effective personal leadership style.

1

LEADERSHIP WE CAN BELIEVE IN

I cannot understand you Australians. Once our
tanks got through in Poland, France and Belgium,
the enemy took it for granted that they were beaten.
But you are like demons. The tanks break through
but your infantry keep fighting.

A German officer taken prisoner at Tobruk in 1941

A key finding of the 1995 Karpin Report was that a
few fundamental management practices go a long
way to improving the effectiveness of leaders and
their impact on performance. Twenty years later, we
find that the leadership fundamentals, in particular
communication, still matter.

Centre for Workplace Leadership,
University of Melbourne, 2016

The capability multiplier

Australia's military consistently punches above its weight.

Thus in 1918 the Australian Corps, operating as a national force for the first time, spearheaded a vital breakthrough on the Western Front; in 1941 the raw 9th Division held Rommel's Afrika Corps at bay at Tobruk; and in 1942 'those ragged bloody heroes' on the Kokoda Track halted the Japanese advance. An Australian battalion group won a strategically significant battle against the Chinese at Kapyong in Korea in 1951; and the newly formed Australian Regular Army mastered counterinsurgency warfare in Malaya, Borneo and Vietnam during the 1950s, '60s and '70s. In 1999 it emerged from two decades of very little operational 'match practice' to play a major role in bringing stability to Timor-Leste. And our forces in the Middle East are now engaged in the longest and most complex war in our history, all the while remaining alert for assignment to disaster relief, anti-terrorism tasks and whatever else the nation asks of them.

This is no less true on the cultural front. For example, the Australian Defence Force was well ahead of the corporate world in extending equal pay for equal work and in opening up almost all its employment categories to women in the early 1980s (the process was completed recently by opening frontline combat opportunities for women). And when, in 2011, it was confronted with damning evidence of sexual harassment, it responded promptly and appropriately, in stark contrast to the evasive measures employed by many other institutions.

At the core of all such achievements is our military's approach to leadership. This was developed more than a century ago by fusing national values with the imperatives of war-fighting. Fine-tuned by each successive generation, it is now embedded as a way of both practising and thinking about leadership—a leadership *culture*—that is not only distinctively Australian but also ticks all the boxes that define contemporary best practice.

It's a striking example of Prussian military theorist von Clausewitz's principle of using natural assets to create inherent advantage.

Leadership when it counts

Imagine yourself in the little town of Marysville in the Central Highlands of Victoria in late February 2009. It's shortly after the devastating bushfires of what has already become known as Black Saturday, a natural disaster that destroyed all but 32 of its 600 buildings and caused the deaths of 35 of its inhabitants.

Uncertainty is rife. Most of the survivors have been temporarily relocated to local towns and villages and, with access to the area now heavily restricted, rumour has it that it might be weeks before you and your fellow citizens will be allowed back.

A public meeting has been called at very short notice. Scores of people are packed into the main room of the only public building left standing. Tired and strained faces can be seen all around. Evidence of the fire can be observed on all sides through the long windows. The smell of smoke still hangs in the air.

The meeting lasts for nearly three hours. Its effect on community morale is profound. One local later told me that she had arrived in very low spirits but had left 'walking on air'.

Much of this effect is due to the actions of one man.

Major General John Cantwell is on loan from the Army to serve in the Victorian Bushfire Reconstruction and Recovery Authority.

He and philanthropist–mining magnate Andrew Forrest had spent the previous day touring the district. Impressed by what they had seen and heard, they had requested a public meeting be organised for the following evening. Now they are here to address it.

Cantwell is the very image of the modern major general: fit, slim and dressed in a baggy camouflage uniform. When invited to speak, he takes off his slouch hat, steps away from the lectern and waves away the proffered microphone with the jovial remark that he is used to talking to soldiers in a loud voice and that microphones often 'get in the way'. He briefly introduces himself by relating how he comes from 'humble origins', joined the Army as a private and rose 'through the ranks', has been in war zones, has experienced and is still suffering from PTSD and, like many men, has unwisely declined counselling. He urges all of us to take advantage of the counselling services that will be provided—'Don't be too proud, particularly you blokes.'

Then, calmly and professionally, he outlines the immediate functions of the Recovery Authority: emergency provision of food, supplies and shelter; and cleaning up. He confirms his intention to work through the embryo local community leadership group that accompanied him the day before.

Then he takes questions. For over an hour. The majority of these—coming as they do from still traumatised people—are on mundane local issues. Some he refers to others present that evening, and some to his staff officer, with the promise that he will get back shortly with the answer. But he deals with most of them himself.

And the way he does so is masterful. Every question is treated with equal seriousness. He projects empathy, composure and competence, leaving the audience with the implicit conviction that the right person is in charge; that the situation may be dire but there is a plan for dealing with it; that everybody's needs will be addressed; and that, with him at the helm, and with his commitment to working through the community's representatives, they can take their first confident steps towards recovery.

Leadership secrets of the Australian Army

This book shows how you too can become a leader your people can believe in and—equally importantly—how you can help them believe in themselves.

Improving your ability to lead might be one of the best favours you can do for yourself in an increasingly volatile, uncertain, complex and ambiguous world. Those who are capable of seizing the opportunities that such circumstances offer—or who are simply able to keep their heads above water—are likely to enjoy a career edge.

The same goes for organisations. A recent major study by Melbourne University's Centre for Workplace Leadership showed that few Australian organisations seem to understand leadership basics. Despite the greater focus on the topic, too many regard leadership as something performed by individuals, and most development programs focus on too few people too late in their careers. Moreover, such programs often have disappointing returns on investment. While those who participate in such programs rate their performance relatively highly, the Melbourne University study found that such positive perceptions are often not reflected in the attitudes of those whom they purport to lead. The implications are clear: it's time for a fresh approach, and organisations that can find innovative and reliable ways to lift their leadership game are likely to gain a business advantage.

Meanwhile, valuable lessons from a respected national institution go begging.

And if such lessons sometimes seem 'secret', it's not because the military wants it that way. Rather it's because, having quietly developed an appropriate leadership culture decades ago, it then simply got on with practising 'what works' (how quintessentially Australian!), using principles so deeply ingrained in its cultural psyche that they are taken as self-evident and thus require little explanation or even analysis.

This inadvertent secrecy is not helped by the fact that most civilians' perceptions are shaped by screen images from other countries and eras: steel-jawed leaders gesturing the way forward under fire, generals poring over maps and rapping out orders, and unquestioning obedience imposed by 'discipline'. So it is little wonder that many assume that most decisions in the military are made at the top and then enacted and controlled within rigid hierarchies.

While there is some truth in this perception, it is far from accurate.

Yes: military leadership is authoritative, but this should not be confused with being authoritarian. *Authoritarian* leadership essentially doesn't work in the very situations in which leadership is most needed. But *authoritative* leadership—that is, leadership by people who earn trust by who they are and what they can do—does.

Yes: the military runs itself in a way that is ostensibly hierarchical, but, as explained in later chapters, it does so in ways that use the best features of hierarchy while avoiding most of the disadvantages.

Yes: much of its success is due to the professionalism of its officers and its cadre of officers and senior non-commissioned officers (NCOs), but much also depends on the strong sense of professionalism, identity and teamwork that goes right down to those at its lowest ranks.

Yes: military leaders have certain advantages afforded by the legal and formal authority that accompanies their rank, but legal authority is of marginal benefit in terms of building commitment, helping people to use their initiative, and keeping them alert and plugging along in challenging conditions.

Yes: not everything that the military does has a ready civilian parallel. Many of its core processes are geared to the demanding circumstances of war-fighting. However, there are more similarities between military and civilian life than is generally realised. One of the most telling demonstrations of this was the way in which—as later chapters relate—hundreds of young national servicemen who served a generation ago went on to gain career benefit in a range of civilian fields by applying the values and skills they learned as junior officers.

And yes: not everything about military leadership is perfect. As noted above, our military has much less analytical understanding of what it does in terms of leadership than might be expected. Like any human institution, it has its faults, faults that it can't always explain or diagnose accurately. Leaders and units sometimes perform below expectations, and sometimes they fail; some former military professionals overuse a directive style in their post-service careers; and when specific practices are examined closely, as they were in the 2011/12 investigations into sexual harassment, many instances of poor or unethical performance can be found. However, just as in that particular instance, when confronted with evidence of poor performance our military invariably takes prompt corrective action that often begins at the top.

Military leadership culture

The leadership principles from which our military's performance derives are based on a solidly embedded leadership culture: a culture that, like other aspects of organisational culture, comes from shared thinking, shared identity and shared assumptions about the 'right thing' to do.

The essence of this leadership culture can be discerned in the three drumbeats that echo throughout the book.

- *Professionalism*: The skill and character displayed by leaders at all levels are expressed in the versatility and competence that are the basis for their inherent authority.
- *Teamwork*: The military's tight teamwork at both micro and macro levels not only builds individual and group engagement but is also an important factor in the adaptability with which units and larger formations organise and run operations.
- *Ethos*: At the core of military leadership culture is an attitude of mind—a way of thinking about oneself and one's duties, and a commitment to professionalism and service.

Think of this leadership culture as an iceberg. The professionalism with which our military tackles whatever it is tasked to do is clearly discernible 'above the surface'. However, its teamwork is much less so, and even then is usually detectable only by a well-honed eye. And the values and ways of thinking that are fundamental to its leadership ethos—qualities embedded in people's hearts and souls—are deeper still, becoming evident only at times, such as when senior people like Lieutenant General David Morrison call out unacceptable professional behaviour, or when relatively junior people are honoured for exceptional and often heroic actions in the service of their team, their institution and their country.

Like an iceberg, this leadership culture simply wouldn't float without the contribution of all three components. Its professionalism and leadership ethos encourages leaders at all levels to step forward to lead, and its teamwork enables the vital 'teams of teams' approach used on operations. The combined effects are powerful indeed.

The argument that follows

This book is based on more than half a century's observations of leadership practices in the Australian Defence Force. The focus is on the ground forces—the Army—but it does not neglect the Navy and the Air Force. In any case, the broad approaches to leadership in all three services are essentially the same.

The chapters that follow are packed with examples, both military and civilian. I draw from historical and contemporary examples of current and recent former service personnel, as well as from research. This began during my assignments as a consultant-in-uniform in the mid-1970s and continued into my civilian careers of scholar and consultant. It culminated in the scores of interviews completed specifically for this book, many with former national servicemen who served as junior officers in the 1960s and '70s, including a deputy prime minister, a state premier, a Supreme Court judge and many successful senior executives and professionals.

Chapters 2 and 3 set the scene. Chapter 2 introduces the concepts of 'leaders' and 'leadership', and explains the cultural foundations of our military's distinctively 'Australian' way of leading and why it is so well suited to the challenges of contemporary operations. Chapter 3 explains how leaders at different levels view these concepts, and outlines the basic elements of the Army's methodology for adaptable leadership on operations.

Chapter 4 examines the leadership ethos that is at the core of military leadership culture, and shows how and why it shapes behaviour and values.

Chapters 5 to 8 explain the Army's team leadership style, as expressed by the '3Rs of leadership'. Chapter 5 gives an overview of the 3Rs model, with Chapters 6, 7 and 8 then successively dealing with its three main elements: Representing (earning trust by being someone the team can believe in); Relating (building self-belief and team spirit through interpersonal leader–follower connections); and Running the team (making the process of working with you intrinsically satisfying as well as productive).

Chapter 9 rounds off our examination by explaining the core principles that guide leadership development. Chapter 10 draws the threads together and suggests some ways in which you and your organisation can put them into effect.

The focus throughout is on what works rather than on what doesn't. I have found leadership to be analogous to the phenomena that prompted Tolstoy's observation in *Anna Karenina*: 'Happy families are all alike; every unhappy family is unhappy in its own way'. That is, good leaders, whatever their context, tend to lead in similar ways and in accordance with similar principles, while poor ones are usually prone to a multitude of misguided and careless behaviours. In any case, most of these poor behaviours have little to do with what we understand to be 'leadership'. We thus learn much more from studying the good leaders than we do from picking over the mistakes of the also-rans.

There are two supporting appendices and a glossary of frequently used terms. Appendix 1 summarises the structure of the contemporary military, in terms of ranks, organisations and major functions. Appendix 2 outlines some of the core professional techniques used for decision-making, tasking and communicating.

I have avoided academic-style referencing within the text itself, with the details of various sources and references appearing chapter-by-chapter at the end of the book. When quoted, currently-serving personnel who are cited are referred to by their rank and a military alphabetical designation, except when the relevant information is on the public record. They run from Lieutenant Commander Alpha through to Flight Lieutenant Mike.

Onwards

In a remarkably short time, Major General John Cantwell established himself as a leader the people of Marysville could believe in. He did so by personifying what the locals were looking for in someone who could lead the recovery. He projected both competence and concern for them as individuals and as a community. To cap it all off, he came across as an ordinary bloke: when the locals looked at him, they saw an idealised reflection of themselves.

The Marysvillians probably thought that Cantwell was unusually talented and, by normal standards, he was. But by the standards of his profession, he wasn't. He was simply doing what had become habitual after so many years within a culture that encourages people at all levels to *lead*, with all the connotations that the term entails.

What would be the benefits to your organisation of having an equivalent leadership culture across all levels of management or, better still, across all levels of the organisation? What if embryo managers were groomed to think of themselves as leaders from an early career stage, and were then progressively developed in terms of skills and outlook? What if all managers practised ways of leading that were guaranteed to not just elicit the best from their teams but also encourage those teams to support other teams in the organisation? And what might *you* have to do—as an individual and as an organisation—to make this happen?

Now come and look below the waterline of the leadership iceberg to learn the 'secrets' of Australian military leadership culture.

2

LEADERSHIP, CULTURE AND CONTEXT

Your Excellency, on behalf of a grateful Army, we
accept this banner with pride and honour. And
to you and all Australians I say, on behalf of all
Diggers: thanks, mate.

Regimental Sergeant Major of the Army Peter
Rosemond, CSC, OAM, to Governor-General
Sir William Deane, AC, KBE, QC, 2001

Intelligent, physically superior, adaptable, imaginative
and brave, easy to lead but difficult to drive, the
Australian soldier was proof that individualism
is the best and not the worst foundation upon
which to build collective discipline.

General Sir John Monash, GCMG, KCB, VD,
Commander of the Australian Corps on the
Western Front

Situational leadership

During the early campaigns of the 'Coalition of the Willing' in early 2002, Major Jon (Irish) Hawkins' Special Forces squadron was tasked with liaising with Afghan Northern Alliance elements. Success depended on winning the trust of local Afghan commanders. With the squadron stretched to its limits, most of the day-to-day liaison activities were delegated to small teams of junior soldiers, usually led by corporals.

These junior teams operated semi-autonomously, with an effectiveness that had much to do with their consistently professional approach to a number of comparatively minor activities that in combination added up to something significant. Thus the teams were scrupulous in consistently and reliably identifying Al-Qaeda elements prior to engaging with them; they treated local villagers fairly by using the local rate when paying for items so they wouldn't adversely affect the local economy; they respected the villagers' livestock; and they ensured local women and children safe passage through combat engagements.

In these and a host of other activities, the Australians exhibited what the Afghan commanders recognised as being the essence of trustworthiness: something on which the locals placed great weight.

The teams were run using an inclusive, pragmatic, compassionate and egalitarian style of leadership has been characteristic of Australian forces throughout our military's short history. It was embedded over a century ago, not just because it was consistent with Australian ways of thinking but—much more importantly—because it worked.

This chapter establishes some working concepts of the Australian military's approach to leadership. It shows how its perceptions and practices evolved from very deep cultural roots—with national historical factors contributing to a form of leadership that is well matched to our no-BS culture—and how well such an approach fits with our military's current operations.

Leadership, leaders and followership

Even though leadership is one of the social sciences' most examined phenomena, it remains difficult to pin down conceptually. It took me a lot of study and consideration to identify and clarify what I regard as its three key elements.

These three elements are defined as follows:

- *Leadership*: a process by which a person or a small group pursues a goal by engaging the concerted efforts of willing followers, in conditions of risk or uncertainty.
- *Leaders*: those who are able and willing to initiate and sustain leadership.
- *Followership*: the willingness to follow a leader and contribute to the achievement of shared goals.

These definitions capture the core themes that appear in the majority of scholarly works:

- Leadership involves human interaction—notionally between one person and others but, in reality, often with leadership exercised by more than one person.

- Leadership is appropriate in conditions of risk and uncertainty. In a situation that is safe or stable, or where there is a clear indication of what needs to be done, 'leadership' per se is not required. (Such situations require 'management', a concept examined in the next chapter.)
- Leaders must have both the skill and the will to sustain the process through thick and thin.
- Leadership and followership are symbiotic and mutually reinforcing processes. Things are achieved most readily when constructive leaders are matched with willing and able followers.
- Finally, leadership is a *process*: a set of activities that merge into something more powerful than the sum of the various elements.

The concept of values-based leadership adds a further shade of meaning. Values are relatively enduring beliefs about what kind of activities or end-states are preferable to others, in the context of a group or organisation's overall purpose and standards. Values provide a 'moral compass' to guide priorities, choices and behaviour. For example, the Army's values of *courage, initiative, respect* and *teamwork* denote how it wants its people to pursue their objectives and conduct themselves in everyday activities. Leaders whose behaviour is consistent with such values not only help to ensure alignment and consistency between and within teams, but also reinforce the implicit importance of those core values.

Although many people see values-based leadership as being synonymous with ethical leadership, the two are distinct—albeit related—concepts. 'Values' denote what matters to an organisation, whereas 'ethics' represent what matters to society as a whole. Leadership can be values-based without being ethical (as might apply in a criminal gang, for example).

Because 'values' represent the soul of an organisation, they help to ensure consistency of standards regardless of the circumstances. The effectiveness of a values-based approach lies in how well such values are reflected in the organisation as a whole. In order for employees to believe in the sincerity of such values, leadership teams at every level must consistently embody them in their own everyday behaviour.

The leadership process—whether values-based or not—typically works as follows:

- It begins with a leader gaining acceptance and trust by being a certain kind of person and by tackling tasks in ways that seem likely to succeed.
- Initial trust is strengthened when the leader spends time and effort building supportive relationships with group members and a sense of unity and cohesion with the team itself.
- All this contributes to a sense of teamwork—a sense of shared identity, purpose and values that is intrinsically satisfying and further adds to the spirit of followership.
- The teamwork effect is even more powerful when such spirit extends to the organisation of which that team is a part.
- As followers' self-esteem, confidence and sense of unity grow, team members engage more strongly with the team and its work, and pay even closer attention to that leader's ideas and approaches.
- All this is subject to a collective contagion/reinforcement effect, whereby team members who see their peers making

the same kinds of adjustments are thereby strengthened in their own good habits.

The process taps into a number of psychological effects—effects with often deep cultural roots that have shaped both their general forms and the way they are commonly practised in specific societies.

Fair dinkum leadership for a no-BS culture

Chapter 1 related how Major General John Cantwell won the trust of the citizens of Marysville in the days following the devastating Black Saturday bushfires. Much of his success was due to the many ways in which his low key and pragmatic leadership style fitted perfectly with the cultural mores that personify Australian culture and society.

Leadership and human evolution

The fundamental values that drive human societies have evolved from more than two million years of living in small communities. In those communities there were essentially two kinds of people: those who were in the tribe and those who were not; or, to put it slightly differently, those who shared the tribe's interests and those who might want to take those interests from it. Thus 'we became wired for culture', as evolutionist Professor Mark Pagel of the University of Reading puts it: instinctively attuned to the values and norms of 'our' group and 'our' tribe. This has given us a strong preference for leaders who look, think and act like us, and who thus can be trusted to look out for our collective interests. Even as societies grew larger and gravitated to cities where tribal interests were just part of a wider agenda for growth and prosperity, people continued to prefer leaders with whom they shared core basic traits.

These evolutionary factors established a deep preference for *identity leadership*: for leaders who were not only technically competent but could also build a sense of shared identity and unity—a broader tribalism—that would drive the collaborative spirit that is key to survival and prosperity. We have evolved to prefer leaders who are patently 'of us, for us, and with us'.

Leadership and national evolution

The definition of 'us' is shaped by deeply rooted identity markers that emerge as national cultures evolve. Many of these identity markers are reflected in cultural narratives: the stories we tell ourselves about ourselves, and which powerfully shape our sense of who we are and how we should behave towards each other.

The narrative for mainstream Australia goes back to the late eighteenth and early nineteenth centuries, when the members of an expanding society had to learn to work together in tackling the task of colonisation. This meant sharing challenges as well as opportunities, and early Australian society thus became imbued with a twin sense of independence and collaboration. These traits continue to be reflected in fundamental values such as 'give it a go', pragmatism, egalitarianism, 'mateship' and a 'fair go'—values that became so deeply embedded that they continued to hold sway long after we became one of the most urbanised nations in the world.

In his book, *Australian History in 7 Questions*, historian John Hirst shows that the process began almost immediately after British settlement in 1788. Hirst argues that the settlement soon became less 'a penal colony' than 'a colony of convicts' in which, from the earliest days of white settlement, convicts were frequently used as overseers, police and for various professional functions, and were assigned the appropriate societal status in each case. In fact, the second governor, Captain John Hunter, told the British government 'to stop looking for eligible free people [because] whatever he wanted doing, there was a convict who could do it'. The social mores that evolved from such practices were cemented by a combination of events that ranged from the increasing liberalism of successive British governments of the era to the economic and political opportunities triggered by the expanding frontier and the gold rushes of the nineteenth century.

All such factors created a national society that favours inclusive, supportive and egalitarian relationships, and demands 'no-BS' leadership from leaders skilled in collaboration as well as problem-solving. 'There is no place for difference in the Australian book of etiquette', says journalist Nick Cater in *The Lucky Culture and the Rise of an Australian Ruling Class*. While inheritance of wealth is 'tolerated', 'no one inherits privilege, and respect is not for sale at any price'. Like historian Hirst, Cater sees Australians as a people who don't mind authori*tative*—as opposed to authori*tarian* —leadership, but who also rarely hesitate to question directions that don't make sense, and respond most positively when they believe that those in authority appreciate community perspectives and will serve the common interests. A culture, in short, in which its Army's senior NCO could use the expression 'mate' when addressing the governor-general to express respect and affiliation rather than over-familiarity.

This would have come as no surprise to those who were tasked more than a century ago with assembling forces for the expeditionary campaigns of the Boer War and World War I. They were recruiting from a society that was already expressing clear preferences for practical and egalitarian leadership. To their credit, those leaders took this as an opportunity and, by melding the imperatives of wartime leadership with the distinctive features of Australian society—a society in which every Jack regarded himself as being as good as his master—they lit the spark for that 'special something' that has imbued the Australian military ever since.

This spirit would have been reinforced by the all-volunteer nature of the First Australian Imperial Force (1st AIF). The Australian military was one of only two armed forces engaged in the Great War that never included conscripts (the other being that of South Africa). The 1916 national referendum on conscription was narrowly decided in favour of the 'no' case and, although there was no way of knowing for certain how the AIF voted, it is generally assumed that those in France voted against conscription, while those in the Middle East and in base areas, where conditions were less extreme and casualties far lower, voted for it. Those who faced the greatest challenges saw themselves as independent and would have wanted to be led on those terms.

The effects of doing so are reflected in the observations of veterans and historians of the Great War, summed up well by the former Australian officer who wrote that

> The only way to manage Australians and to get the best out of them is to take them fully into one's confidence. 'Here is the job,' we [officers] would say; 'when it is done we can go home'. Even though the work was triple, that calculated as a fair thing, and it would be completed ahead of schedule.

These pragmatic and egalitarian practices are confirmed by research on Australian writing from the Great War by historian Clare Rhoden of Melbourne University. Soldiers of the 1st AIF were willing to follow their officers in pursuit of sensible goals, but were 'less ready to comply with activities perceived as extraneous'. They might have been difficult to handle off duty but they were excellent soldiers.

The continued influence of egalitarian norms is demonstrated by the behaviour of POWs in a Japanese prison camp a generation later.

> You might have imagined that if human beings were worked hard and beaten to the point of death, they would be reduced to barely functional skeletons, scraps of biology, with all the so-called veneer of civilisation flayed out of them, all national culture and character trampled out of them. Not so. The prisoners of the Japanese remained inextinguishably American, Australian, British, Dutch. The Americans were the great individualists of the camps, the capitalists, the cowboys, the gangsters. The British hung on to their class structure like bulldogs, for grim death. The Australians kept trying to construct little male-bonded welfare states ... Within their little tribes, rice went back and forth all the time, but this was not trading in commodities futures, it was sharing, it was Australian tribalism.

Numerous other accounts from historical and contemporary sources illustrate the point. Australians are egalitarian and supportive by nature and, led in ways that align with those values, they are capable of exceptional levels of performance and teamwork.

Any Australian leader who ignores this principle is not only asking for trouble but also ignoring a crucial resource.

Leadership and the contemporary scene

The conclusions of evolutionists and historians are supported by the recent findings of an ongoing series of qualitative and expert-panel investigations, initiated in the early 1990s to investigate national perspectives on 'quality' and 'leadership'. Known as the Australian Cultural Imprints Studies (ACIS), it was commissioned and sponsored by a consortium of government agencies and industry groups.

One of the study's most important findings reflects the cultural factors outlined above. Australians prefer a leadership style that ACIS labelled the 'Captain-Coach': authoritative but affiliative and egalitarian; focused on the common interest; leading by example; and, 'most importantly, sharing the pain'. This contrasts with what ACIS calls the 'Taskmaster', whose focus is on task outcomes regardless of team welfare, and the 'Patrician', who attends to team welfare but behaves like the social superior of those being led.

The ACIS studies regarded the captain-coach style as 'imperative' for sparking the engagement and discretionary effort that is essential for implementing quality.

In short, an authoritative and inclusive leadership style is not only what Australians respond best to but also what works best in terms of business improvement.

The operational context: Adapting to adaptability

The need to get the most from limited resources has never been more pressing than in the contemporary operational context. It is a context marked by novel issues and disruptive technology. The military refers to this as a 'VUCA' environment, an acronym that stands for volatility, uncertainty, complexity and ambiguity.

The organisational and professional adaptability required for VUCA operations comes partly from the skills of commanders and their staffs at all levels, and partly from an approach to organising that relies heavily on good team leadership at all levels.

Brigadier Shane Gabriel commanded Australia's Mentoring and Reconstruction Task Force in Afghanistan in 2008–9. He ran his unit on the basis that every individual engaged in such operations, no matter how junior, had to be prepared to take on far more responsibility for mission success than would have been expected in 'more traditional and conventional operations'. This meant that leaders at all levels had to keep one eye on the ball and the other on the broader field, and this, as much as anything else, requires delegation of authority for day-to-day activities as far down the chain as possible.

Military organisations in contemporary operations must be prepared for a wide range of contingencies and be able to switch readily from one to the other. A common expression used to describe contemporary operations is 'the Three Block War'. This denotes a situation in which a single unit must be prepared to engage simultaneously in armed conflict in a first block, provide support and mentoring for indigenous forces in a second, and help with community rebuilding in a third. All the while, the unit must be able to switch seamlessly between each set of activities, and operate within each block in ways that support the other two.

Thus an infantry company in Afghanistan might be detached to guard a vital installation this week, take on mentoring duties with the Afghan Army next week, and then commence patrolling duties a week or so after that. Each of its platoons and sections must be able to perform these varied tasks at short notice, either independently or in conjunction with other units and sub-units, such as cavalry, artillery, engineers and logistics. And, not least, it must be able to work with elements of the local population, so all soldiers must be appropriately skilled in cross-cultural competence.

Recent history suggests that this is something for which the Australian military seems to have a natural bent. In describing Australian soldiers' strengths in cross-cultural competence and compassion, military historians refer to this talent as the facility for 'taking the principles of war and applying them to peace'. The expression was coined to describe Australian military support activities in Somalia in 1993, when the defence force was tasked with keeping the peace during a particularly terrible time in that African nation's history. Historians now regard what those soldiers did as 'exceptional'. Their mission did not require them to rebuild warehouses or schools or jails; to assist with the town water supply; to move containers all over town so that other relief agencies could have secure stores; to build playground equipment for orphanages; or to help tribal elders arbitrate on domestic issues. But they did all these things and more, instinctively recognising that 'peacekeeping' required as much attention to rebuilding community structure, social capital and spirit as it did to protecting a vulnerable society from unscrupulous irregular forces.

A decade later we see a similar sentiment expressed by a civilian who wrote to the newspapers to praise those 'pussycats with guts'.

We sent a modern disciplined army to Timor but an army which carried in its heart the values of our liberal democracy . . . The same

25

men who stood their ground in the dangerous ridges and valleys along the western border defending unfamiliar territory could, a week later, be seen putting up water tanks in orphanages and having their photos taken with children ... Time and time again I heard ... Timorese in all walks of life, in words or by thumbs-up sign language, praise the Australian army's professionalism and humanity.

A final example is the one that opened this chapter: the special forces squadron at the beginning of what has proved to be an ongoing commitment in Afghanistan. The readiness and skill with which our forces apply these principles in contemporary operations owe much not only to their professionalism and versatility but also to the cultural drivers of an 'Australian way' of leadership.

Onwards

With these opening chapters as our foundation, we are now ready to analyse our military's way of leading. This begins with a brief examination of military perspectives on leadership, including how these facilitate the adaptable team-of-teams approach that enables our forces to be flexible and agile in the contemporary battlespace.

We will see that, far from impeding military effectiveness, the egalitarian and pragmatic values of Australian society have consistently proven to be an asset.

3

LOOKING AT LEADERSHIP

Managers are necessary; leaders are essential.

Field Marshal Sir William Slim,
KG, GCB, GCMG, GCVO, GBE, DSO, MC, KStJ

Warfare today is changing faster and on a larger
scale than at any time in the last 350 years . . .
At the heart of this phenomenon lies not a
military evolution but a political, social, and
moral revolution.

William S. Lind & Gregory A. Thiele,
4th Generation Warfare Handbook, 2015

Fighting spirit, enterprise and leadership

One of the essential elements of military capability is 'fighting spirit'. Such spirit derives from morale, resilience, skills, social bonds and cohesion, as well as from the *esprit de corps* that comes from identification with, and pride in, the legacies of past achievements.

Leadership is the thread that links these key factors: 'leadership' as both a widely practised style of *behaving* and a distinctive way of *thinking*. To understand Australian Army leadership—indeed, to understand the Army—you have to understand this thinking and what lies behind it.

When former Lieutenant Colonel Colin Toll took over as the general manager of the Mount Blue Cow ski resort in the late 1980s, its owners gave him three years to make it profitable. To many, it would have seemed 'a big ask'. Mount Blue Cow was a small, newly established operation in an area dominated by the two big established resorts of Perisher and Thredbo. However, Colin quickly identified his critical potential edge. With an increasing number of families coming to the area to ski each year, he intended to compete on the basis of improved customer service. Mount Blue Cow would become 'the family-friendly resort'.

Staff culture was at once both his biggest challenge and best opportunity. Improvements to customer service would require focus on a host of comparatively minor interactions between customers and frontline resort staff, as the common attitude of ski-industry employees to the skiing public at the time was one of polite condescension. Most employees were casuals, motivated primarily by the opportunity to ski during their time off, with no particular incentive to treat their customers differently just because the boss said so.

To achieve his goal, Colin would have to get his employees to see their roles in a different light and behave accordingly.

Colin did so by drawing on principles that had served him well in his military career. Just as with the young troopers in his armoured squadrons, he had every confidence that the resort employees would respond well to both being treated seriously and tackling a worthwhile challenge 'in good company'.

He began by calling them in for a number of interactive team sessions a week before the ski season officially started. In these, Colin challenged his various teams—lift-hands, food-outlet staff and ticket sellers—to explore what each could do to improve their own interactions with customers as well as support other functions in doing so. 'You know your local situation much better than I do,' he told them, 'so you're more likely to come up with the right answers.' Through their participation in this process, employees realised that a different approach would not only involve little more effort but would possibly be more fun and eventually more satisfying. And their very involvement helped to lift engagement and team spirit.

Meanwhile—being not so naive as to expect he could get this done without some tangible incentives—Colin made it known that those who performed well would have a guaranteed job at the resort in the following season and would also be helped to find jobs in overseas resorts during the off-season if they so desired.

Once the season got going, Colin initiated various activities to make people feel part of 'Team Blue Cow'. He ran a weekly staff social event in which milestones and personal events such as birthdays were celebrated, and where he presented and discussed weekly progress indicators as well as market-research feedback gathered from skiers. Colin would talk about positive incidents of customer service he had observed during the week (while doing what he called 'management-by-skiing-around'). And during his daily interactions with the frontline, he would express his appreciation for what his employees were doing, and subtly reiterate the overall strategy in terms of the specific role of that given team. Morale at the resort had never been higher.

Grassroots perspectives on leadership

The approach that Colin Toll took in tackling his business challenge is consistent with both the captain-coach leadership style introduced in the previous chapter and the perspectives of currently serving junior officers, sergeants and corporals whom I consulted as part of a recent study of Army leadership.

These junior leaders had observed how effective leaders get people to work together willingly and collaboratively by their:

- *Expertise*: Knowing their stuff, with knowledge, perspective and experience that 'made us feel that they are always on top of things'.
- *Character*: Being calm, steady and focused at all times, 'not set back by setbacks', and showing that 'they trusted their teams to deal with whatever the situation threw at them'.
- *Intentions*: Focusing attention on clear goals, and 'making me feel part of something that really mattered, rather than just doing a job'.
- *Communication*: Communicating their intentions in language that 'makes sense to those at our level'.

- *Engagement*: Generating trust by being 'engaging and personal', 'open to ideas about improving tasking and processes', 'making team members feel that their views are valued' and 'bouncing ideas off their NCOs'.
- *Team management*: Spreading the workload by appropriate delegation, so team members could 'get on with the nitty-gritty while they concentrated on the bigger picture', particularly in teams in which 'most of us have gone around the block a few times'.

The psychological effects of being led this way include feelings of:

- *Unity and agency*: 'It's a great feeling to be working in a well knit team'; 'we appreciated being treated as colleagues rather than as cogs in the machine'; 'after a while, we got used to trusting the boss's judgement and we would do most things without question'; 'when you know the "why" as well as the "how" you're better able to use your initiative at the right times'; and 'we felt we could do anything with this person in charge'.
- *Purpose and focus*: 'Felt part of a team with a common vision and purpose'; and 'had a strong desire to do my best for the team'.
- *Professional and personal growth*: 'Learned about and improved myself as a professional'; and 'wanted to emulate that leader and rise to his standards'.
- *Intrinsic satisfaction*: 'Looked forward to coming to work each day'; 'even though we were run off our feet, I had a clear idea of what was required and I knew that the boss

was working at least as hard as everybody else'; and—perhaps something that sums it up best—'felt exhausted but successful'.

The officers and NCOs spoke of the importance of leaders who leave their team in better shape when they eventually move on to another appointment (as one put it, 'a leader who doesn't leave a legacy has worked at only half capacity'). Good leaders do this, they said, regardless of the extra effort, with the really skilled ones managing their teams in ways that achieve goals while simultaneously stretching and developing team members individually and collectively.

Don't, however, get the impression that these service members thought Australian military leadership was near-perfect—they had plenty of criticisms on the leadership front. But what was striking was the nature of such comments. The large majority were about behaviours that were not actually 'leadership' as defined. Most involved dodging or otherwise neglecting the responsibilities of leadership: micromanagement; inability or unwillingness to engage with followers; lack of confidence; failure to see or explain the bigger picture or to show where team activities fitted within this bigger picture; too much time 'ticking boxes'; interpersonal aloofness; and the like. All such behaviours should be avoided by anyone who wants to 'lead', simply because they do not amount to 'leadership'.

The main exception to this is related to 'inauthenticity'. Inauthenticity in a leader was essentially seen as the tendency to prioritise personal goals and personal benefit over those of the team. Relevant negative examples given by grassroots practitioners were of leaders who were driven by career advancement or the desire to boost their own image at the expense of broader interests, or of those who drew back from taking an ethical stance on contentious issues for fear of its effect on their standing with their peers. However, inauthenticity is of a different order to the motivation-sapping behaviours noted above. History provides many examples of self-serving, inauthentic leaders who were very effective in motivating people, even though their morals and motives were questionable. (The next chapter shows that this is one of the reasons why a strong leadership ethos is a crucial foundation for a healthy leadership culture.)

The perspective from the top

Another perspective is provided by a pair of seasoned leadership campaigners, whose views on the subtle differences between leadership and management are particularly insightful.

The textbooks tell us that *management* is an analytical, systematic and methodical process for influencing group behaviour in situations in which there is often a 'best' or 'preferred' method, whereas *leadership* is more interpersonally based and exploratory.

But in practice the distinctions between management and leadership are far from clear.

According to former national serviceman, ex-Victorian premier, community leader and business executive Jeff Kennett, the main difference is in the mindset. The major requirement for a manager is to 'keep things ticking along', he says, whereas leaders take their teams in new directions. For leaders, management is *a* but not *the* priority. Good leaders think about the future and its opportunities through the prism of the present, and, according to Kennett, such thinking is usually only developed 'progressively and gradually'. He recalls 'many good 2ICs who floundered when they were promoted to the top job' because their development as leaders had been left to chance. Years of keeping things ticking along often embed ways of thinking so deeply that people find it hard to shift their mindset—in fact, don't even understand the need to shift—when they reach senior levels. They and their career managers seem to erroneously expect that smart people will somehow acquire leadership skills by osmosis as they advance up the managerial ladder.

Kennett's views are supported by the perspectives of another seasoned campaigner.

Major General Jim Molan, AO, DSC recently retired from a military career in which he led a number of large organisations that included a mix of military and civilian personnel, the highlight being his position as chief of operations in the Multinational Force Headquarters in Iraq during the intense combat operations of 2004–5. He is now a director of several companies and also the Ethics Centre, and he too recently ventured into politics.

In his testimony to the 2009 Victorian Bushfires Royal Commission about Black Saturday, Molan addressed a number of important aspects of leadership, management, teamwork and culture.

He was particularly insightful on the distinctive challenges of leading complex organisations in rapidly shifting situations. Leadership in such situations should not be regarded as a solo effort, he says. Experienced leaders invest time in developing and honing the skills, practices and spirit of their team well in advance of any obvious challenges. They strive to build teams that can help them avoid becoming bogged down in detail and which will be a source of appropriate counsel when the leader needs it. Those supported by such teams are thus better able to find the time and mental capacity for activities that can be achieved only by them: activities such as 'climbing up into the crow's nest' to gauge the bigger picture, getting out to assess and bolster morale, and working upwards and sideways with more senior leaders and counterparts in other parts of the organisation.

This is no less true for the military, says Molan. It is popularly but erroneously believed that military leaders have unquestioned and unchallenged authority, but this is usually far from the case. Military organisations often have complex structures with a variety of skill sets and agendas, and often their civilian elements will not be under the senior military person's direct authority.

You will struggle to get others to follow you in such circumstances, says Jim Molan, if you are not skilled in coordinating and focusing—that is, in *managing*—the various elements in order to get the best from each. Whatever the context, therefore, sound leadership usually depends in part on sound management. For example, however strong the spark of enterprise that Colin Toll lit in his people, he would have had little bottom-line effect if he and his senior colleagues were not also skilled and experienced in the basic activities associated with running that type of organisation.

But even the management process will not compensate for lack of leadership. As Field Marshal William Slim, legendary World War II commander and former Australian governor-general, put it neatly in the epigraph at the beginning of this chapter, 'Managers are necessary; leaders are essential'.

Military leadership in action

'It went like a military operation.' It's an expression sometimes used to describe the outcome of complicated and interrelated activities that achieve a desired result in the desired time, regardless of unplanned hitches.

Civilians often assume that this is achieved by close top-down direction and strict discipline, with the military leader seen as analogous to a conductor of a symphony orchestra, with the players following the score according to interpretation and direction from the podium. The stereotype is of the *leader as controller*, overseeing and directing all that goes on.

Those familiar with the military know better. They know that a more relevant metaphor would be a jazz band in which a handful of players works *with*—as opposed to work *to*—a central theme, sometimes in unison and sometimes improvising, with the group leader exercising loose overall control. In short, the *leader-as-catalyst*: overseeing and managing the total process, in marked contrast to the controller model, but acting very much as an inclusive energiser/facilitator to help others get things done.

The organisational form by which military forces achieve this adaptability is 'networked hierarchy'. This is an approach to organising that benefits from a hierarchical structure's inherent simplicity and responsiveness, while avoiding the narrowness of stove-piping. ('Stove-piping' refers to a structure that restricts interactions and information flow between different parts of an organisation, in which collaboration and information exchange generally either happen only at the top or require top-level clearance.)

Within a networked hierarchy, the focus for action and decision-making will vary according to the situation. A military force is regarded as a set of 'building blocks', in which the precise configuration is determined by the task and situation. These blocks can be arranged in a variety of groupings, all of which enable those at the apex and the nodes to run the overall process. The configuration can be changed if and when the task changes, with effort directed when, where and how it is needed.

Networked hierarchies typically comprise teams of teams, with the small teams operating as the building blocks of the larger configuration. Those in each team draw much of their energy from their identification with that specific team and its leader, but they also draw part of their purpose and sense of identity with those in other teams and the larger entity.

Thus the force assembled for a combat task might be grouped around an infantry battalion, with an artillery battery to provide fire support, armoured personnel carriers and tanks to enhance mobility and firepower, and a combat engineer troop for specialist tasks. With that combat mission achieved, the battalion might—in the spirit of the Three Block War metaphor in Chapter 2—switch its focus to mentoring local forces. Since it will then need a lesser level of mobility and firepower, the various support elements can be reallocated or scaled down. In both cases, the force will readily take an appropriate configuration, with overall command still exercised through the battalion headquarters. With everyone using the same professional terminology, sharing the same professional values and being familiar with the capabilities of each of the various elements, the focus and effort will move seamlessly with each change in task and grouping.

The appropriate approach to leadership in such a configuration is the leader-as-catalyst mode introduced above. Rather than directing activities in detail, such leaders facilitate the performance of others. They act as the nodes or centres of networks of organisational relationships—as focal agents who help others to make sense of and respond to what is going on, all the while being alert to the need to take closer control in crises or emergencies. At the same time, they and their subordinate leaders will be continuously and collaboratively exploring the unfolding situation for implications and lessons that might have relevance to the operations of both today and tomorrow.

This adaptable operational leadership process has many advantages. As an organisational form, it facilitates coordination between different elements, keeps the important decision-making points close to where they will be enacted, and makes it possible to readily shift the focus from one task to another. As a channel for leadership, it taps the collective resources within the network, provides a broad source of information for decision-making, and frees up leaders at each level to focus on and manage external relationships as well as opportunities and threats. And as a means of building human capital, a networked hierarchy stimulates team development, deepens followership and—by no means least—broadens the leadership repertoire and capacity of all those within the network.

Onwards

As the season at Mount Blue Cow progressed, there was a noticeable shift in mood at the resort. Skiers—even those without families—felt more comfortable and, sensing this, staff tried even harder to serve their customers well. Group cohesion improved and, as lift-hands, food-outlet staff and ticket-sellers all grew accustomed to a stronger service focus, skier numbers climbed while those of adjacent resorts remained flat. Everyone felt like a winner, and morale soared. Despite comparatively poor skiing conditions across the region, Mount Blue Cow enjoyed its most profitable year ever, a result that was repeated in the next season and the one after that. Four years later its nearest competitor made a successful takeover bid, and Mount Blue Cow is now part of the Perisher complex.

Perhaps most tellingly, the notion of 'customer service' has become the norm in the New South Wales skiing industry. Colin Toll has long since moved on but his legacy remains.

At first glance, military operations might seem to have few obvious civilian parallels. However, as with its corporate cousins, the military must continually deal with disruptive competition and the need to align a range of frontline processes with goals that are continuously varying. Its consistent success in meeting such challenges is due to its ability to merge and align its leadership practices with appropriate organisational forms and tactics, with many of its most important tasks carried out by small versatile teams that collaborate and support each other.

We see the essence of this approach in how Colin Toll led his teams to reach beyond themselves for worthwhile goals. By treating his people as valued colleagues, building meaning and focus by involving them in the process, forging a sense of common identity and lifting their belief that *we* can do it, he led them into a different way of working.

Keep those factors in mind. In a slightly different form, they are going to appear again and again in this book.

4

THE MILITARY LEADERSHIP ETHOS

The day after graduation, we went to the Sergeants'
Mess for drinks and I remember vividly how I felt
when these hard men called me 'Sir' for the first
time. That was when it really hit me that I now had
some fairly serious responsibilities to live up to.

David Gillett, retired career soldier, reflecting on his
final day in 1964 at the Officer Cadet School, Portsea

I'm an Australian soldier who is an expert in close combat
I am physically and mentally tough, compassionate and courageous
I lead by example, I strive to take the initiative
I am committed to learning and working for the team
I believe in trust, loyalty and respect for my Country, my mates
and the Army
The Rising Sun is my badge of honour
I am an Australian Soldier—always

The Australian Army's 'Contract with Australia', 2016

A way of behaving, thinking and self-definition

Gerard Windsor's book, *All Day Long the Noise of Battle: An Australian attack in Vietnam*, relates an action fought by an infantry company group during the 1968 Tet Offensive. Windsor's interest was sparked not only because such a relatively significant incident had gone largely unreported but also because an old friend, Mark Maloney, had commanded one of the platoons involved.

Windsor wrote to Maloney, telling him that he had been 'enormously moved' by what the platoon had done, and wanted to write about it. But when Maloney phoned a few days later, he set some firm guidelines for his former schoolmate. 'I don't want you writing about me,' he told Windsor. 'You can write about the diggers. But not about me.'

These words, says Windsor, gave him

> an inkling of a world anchored by the two pillars of hierarchy and honour. A hierarchy of officers and soldiers, a hierarchy that meant not only authority and responsibility but also solicitude and care . . . More gradually I came to see a code of honour. Officers are conscious of themselves as servants of the nation . . . Hierarchy and honour mesh in a particularly noticeable way when it comes to the history/mythology of an individual unit or regiment.

The military's leadership ethos has rarely been articulated so well.

It's an expression of professional responsibility, based on two related principles: officers' first priorities are to *service* and to *team*, and the most important competencies in their professional portfolio are those associated with 'leadership'.

Such an ethos has moral as well as practical roots. The profession and its members must be able to rely on leaders at all levels to do the right thing and do it right. Further, committing to such an ethos is an important moral stepping stone for accepting the personal responsibilities of leadership.

This chapter examines the essentials of this ethos. It shows how this way of thinking has shaped the long-term career behaviour of so many individuals, both as soldiers and as civilians; discusses the practical and memorable motto by which our military expresses its principles; and finishes by explaining how adhering to such an ethos prevents egos getting in the way of responsibilities.

Testaments to success: Seven not-so-little Australians

Ernie Bryon, Peter Graham, Terry Earle, Tim Fischer, Jeff Kennett, John McCallum and Colin Chapman. A tiny handful of the young Australians who took on the challenge of officership after being called up for national service in the late 1960s and early '70s, and whose lives were significantly shaped by the experience. Bryon and Graham rose to senior corporate executive positions, Earle went from corporate success to small-business success, Fischer and Kennett distinguished themselves in politics, and McCallum and Chapman had successful academic careers.

Like those of their peers who volunteered, they first attended a 22-week course at the Officer Training Unit at Scheyville, NSW, and then served the balance of their time as junior officers. All emerged from the experience with not only a distinct set of junior executive skills and qualities such as confidence, resilience, focus and determination but also a distinct way of thinking about themselves, particularly that no situation, no matter how difficult, was beyond them. Together with the large majority of other former national service officers who were interviewed for this book, and consistent with a broader and more systematic study of national service officers of that period, they credit this leadership ethos as the springboard for a successful career.

'Foundational' is how Ernie Bryon describes his junior officer training and experience. It gave him decision-making and planning skills together with self-confidence, self-belief and self-discipline, all of which helped to differentiate him from his peers on his return to BHP. He recalls an example that occurred soon after he had taken over the company's local training department. Tasked with expanding the facility, he inadvertently overstepped his authority and was carpeted by his general manager to have his 'wrist slapped'. However, Bryon says, although it had been 'a bit stupid of me, I got credit for using my initiative, especially given BHP's unspoken philosophy of "fix-it-and-then-report-it"; and I got on well with him from then on, so much so that he mentored me from time to time'.

'I can and I will.' This was 'drummed into' Bryon and his peers during his national service experience and was still guiding him decades later, when he experienced some 'dark moments' in making some tough executive decisions. Later in his career, it was one of the main factors he looked for when judging plant managers: he looked for evidence of their willingness to be decisive, to take risks and to involve others when needed; for someone who would 'keep their eye on the goal, would listen to the experts, but could and would ultimately make the call'.

Similarly, Peter Graham's officer training made him realise that he was capable of much more than he had previously imagined.

He vividly recalls how this crystallised on the final training exercise. Tired and run down after ten solid days, Graham had injured his foot and the training staff offered him the chance to pull out. But he was acting as platoon commander and was determined to make it through. He still recalls the deep satisfaction of knowing that 'I did something tough and did it with good mates', and continues to regard this as one of the most significant early experiences in a career that culminated in executive roles in a number of well-known Australian organisations.

When Terry Earle was called up, he was determined to make the most of it. He applied for officer selection in the hope that he would acquire skills he could use later. Returning to the ANZ bank after his service, he quickly rose to executive level. One of the most satisfying events in his banking career happened early in his time as head of the Credit Card division. He was given the task of launching Visa but, with several hundred people reporting to him across Australia, he was unsure of his team's capacity for the task. Then by chance he met a training professional on a long flight to Perth who told him about his leadership development program. Earle had him do 'a trial run' for some of his people, with specific reference to launching Visa, chiefly to identify the extent to which they were capable of acting as leaders and as teams of teams. 'The result was extraordinary,' he says. 'They lapped it up. It was like I had helped to open a different part of their brains beyond their professional core. My division became a really exciting place to work. Just as satisfyingly, the project launched a number of successful careers among many of my people, particularly the women.' But Earle sometimes wonders whether he would have been so willing to take it on had he not been guided by the principles that his military service had instilled in him.

It's a way of thinking that is equally useful in the political arena. Tim Fischer served in Vietnam and fought in the Battle of Fire Support Base Coral during the Tet Offensive in mid-1968. He went on to a political career, becoming leader of the National Party in 1990 and, six years later, deputy prime minister. Officer training and experience helped to pull him out of his comfort zone, putting him under pressure and forcing him 'to learn skills and a lot about tasks and priorities'. He recalls his 'frenetic character-building years in uniform' from which he learned much about managing people and pressure. Such capacity was particularly useful when he was chairing the National Security Committee during the major incident that became known as the Papua New Guinea Sandline affair. In the absence of Prime Minister Howard, Fischer had to lead the process, meeting the challenge of keeping National Security Committee meetings 'focused and oriented on the practicalities'. He remembers with amusement how, when it was all over, he told the assembled senior brass that '2nd Lieutenant Tim Fischer is very grateful for the contribution you have made'.

Jeff Kennett served as a national service infantry officer in Malaysia and Singapore, then worked in the family business before being elected to the Victorian parliament. He served as premier from 1992 to 1999, and continues to be prominent in public and business life. One of the reasons he had been keen to go into national service was his early realisation of the need to master the leadership art: to be put in a situation where 'you have to learn to do it on your own merits, rather than by pulling rank, being friends or winning popularity'. He sees his success as having been due to a strong belief in teamwork, communication, values and individual responsibility, allied with 'meticulous planning' of policies and priorities.

A strong leadership ethos is equally important in other fields. John McCallum and Colin Chapman attained professorial status in their respective academic disciplines, and both credit their officer training for the self-confidence and skills that helped them to lead in their particular areas. McCallum, now director of the National Institute for Dementia Research, feels that his experience as a military leader has given him 'permission to be a certain kind of person at a crucial stage of my life: to be less introspective and more active, and to feel more competent'. He is certain that this gave him a career advantage. 'The confidence I needed for giving direction to a team of experienced soldiers has been so useful subsequently, even though it was a fraction of my life in temporal terms.' When McCallum was appointed deputy vice-chancellor at a major Australian university, he drew on what he had learned in the Army. It helped him to 'think team' and get people working together, and to 'work out who and when to let loose'. All this made the role 'surprisingly easy', not only in giving instructions but also in engaging with and delegating to others.

For his part, one of Chapman's biggest challenges as dean of a pharmacy faculty was maintaining morale and focus during the amalgamation of the autonomous Victorian College of Pharmacy with the much larger and more powerful Monash University. This required good teamwork and communications on the college's side as well as 'fleetness of foot' during the half-dozen years of bedding down the amalgamation. There was also the subsequent challenge of lifting the international status of the faculty so that it could attract top-level teaching and research staff. Now an emeritus professor at Monash University, Chapman is 'still struck' by the leadership qualities and achievements of many of those who did national service. 'It's hard to pinpoint, but I'm sure the man-management and delegation skills, the strategic thinking skills, the need for good reconnaissance and the need for careful planning all helped enormously—not to mention self-discipline.'

Commitment, focus and confidence

Whether it is an implicit code such as 'I can and I will' or the explicit principles within the Australian soldier's covenant to the nation, quoted at the beginning of this chapter, such a way of thinking requires sustained commitment to core values and ways of behaving. It is a way of thinking that significantly shapes how you define yourself to yourself and to others, and how you perceive the obligation associated with your role.

Because this ethos is part of one's self-definition, it is extremely 'sticky', often shaping people's behaviour for the rest of their working lives. For example, although former aviation officer Peter Hewitt served for only a brief time in the Army, he was 'always ready to be the boundary pusher' both in uniform and during his subsequent civilian career. Although Hewitt acknowledges the early career benefits of having 'a certain amount of natural authority', he quickly learned that being a leader is not just about dealing with tasks and problems. You have to engage with your people, he says. 'Show them that you respect their views. Be inclusive. Be fair dinkum. Because in the end, task accomplishment will come down to them.'

Brigadier Roger Noble led one of Australia's first combined-arms units in the contemporary Middle Eastern campaigns. Noble recalls that all the most influential commanding officers (COs) he'd had when he was a junior officer were all 'focused on ensuring that we were better professionals when we left their care'. In that way, he says, 'they not only benefited us: they also made the Army as a whole just that little bit stronger'. The experience cemented his way of thinking about himself and his leadership responsibilities.

The same ethos drives the behaviour of leaders in the other two military services. For example, naval engineer Captain Rachel Durbin, who currently heads a major ship system maintenance program sees the task as coming 'with a huge responsibility and ongoing challenges'. She regards any leadership role in the military as 'a privileged position that is bestowed on you by your followers'. It's an ethos that impels her colleague Lieutenant Commander Alpha to devote most of her working day to a range of people issues, including monitoring training activities, running or attending meetings, and connecting and counselling. But Alpha regards the most important of these as 'simply listening'. She learned the importance of listening from a respected former CO. The clear indication that he was in it for the larger good was not just the time he gave to his people but also how he did so. 'He not only stopped what he was doing and gave you his whole attention but he would then take up many of the issues from such conversations—often despite what we suspected was a certain pushback at more senior levels.' He inspired Alpha's habit of doing most of her paperwork after hours. 'My work time,' she now says, 'belongs to my people.'

A similar example is that of Group Captain Bravo. After a series of audits had pointed to a deep issue in engineering safety, Defence had been put on notice to fix it within two years or be prosecuted. But, with only a handful of requirements having been achieved in the following year, Bravo was tasked to sort it out. He diagnosed the chief problem as coordination difficulties across a complex bureaucracy involving all three services and the public service. Bravo worked closely with and through his small team, setting a 'punishing pace' that team members were comfortable with because of Bravo's professionalism and clear commitment to task success. His total focus was evident: he was always first in and last out each day, and stayed positive despite the challenges. The team achieved all its targets six weeks ahead of schedule. Bravo had told his team that 'we can and we will do it'. And they did.

Although the Army now considers this leadership ethos to be relevant to all levels and ranks, this is essentially a formal recognition of the fundamental cultural truth that was discussed in the previous chapter. Whatever their rank, Australian soldiers have always been ready to 'give it a go' in the interests of the team. Evidence of the effects can be seen in many of the records held in the massive database at the Centre for Army Lessons (CAL) at Puckapunyal in Victoria. For more than a decade, CAL has been gathering information on the experiences of teams and individuals in the Army's various deployments around the world, and, while its main purpose is to identify lessons for future doctrine and practice, it can also detect trends in values and practices. Thus in its archives we can see, for example, a report from senior members of a combat signals regiment on the benefits of giving junior NCOs greater opportunities for leadership and accountability, a practice that is 'paying off handsomely in terms of enhanced trust at all levels and in the greater opportunities for the many junior soldiers who are keen to use their initiative'. Its records also provide evidence of the enhanced confidence of Australian soldiers as they compare themselves favourably with their counterparts in élite units from other countries, such as the US Marine Corps.

All these cases illustrate one of the most important effects of a strong leadership ethos. It helps to build the mental strength and self-confidence needed for stepping into uncertainty and accepting the responsibility of taking others along, undaunted by difficulties and dangers: in short, the resolve to lead from the front, whatever the challenge.

'Mission-team-me': The practical expression of the leadership ethos

In its characteristic pragmatic Australian way, our military expresses its ethos in a simple and practical three-word motto.

Mission-team-me describes a hierarchy of priorities by which military leaders demonstrate their authenticity, morals and professional fitness for their roles. At the top is the mission (or the broader needs of the organisation), after which you should look after the needs of the team. Only then may you attend to 'me'.

Mottos or verbal checklists such as 'I can and I will' and mission-team-me can be important prompts or guides for someone who is tired, stressed, under pressure and longing for a break. By reminding people of their obligations, they help habitualise certain perspectives and ways of behaving—all of which contribute to a strong leadership culture.

The long-term benefits of such an ethos are reflected in the experiences of the former national service officers discussed earlier in the chapter. Peter Graham was one of many who took that belief system with him into corporate life, and it continued to guide him even at senior levels when he might have thought he'd already proved himself. One example was when he was Fairfax

Media's chief operating officer and the company became embroiled in a long industrial dispute in 2003 over the relocation of printing operations from the newspaper's 'Dickensian' Melbourne metropolitan building to a new plant at Tullamarine. Entry to the new plant was blockaded by the print unions, and the local police declined Graham's request to help him and his four-man team enter the plant and complete the commissioning process to get the machinery up and running. So he and his team took matters into their own hands. 'We reconnoitred the site, found a spot in the fence away from the blockaded gate, and popped up on the inside, to the astonishment and embarrassment of the police who were there.' Then they set about completing the commissioning process. Because it was essentially technical, it required no direct involvement from Graham, but he had learned that there were other things a leader should do to support his team in such situations. So he made coffee and sandwiches and performed various other menial tasks to enable his team to concentrate on the task at hand. He learned later that his team regarded his leadership as having been 'critical' in maintaining focus and confidence during what had been a testing time.

Years later Graham recalls the experience as a reminder of the values needed for good people management, particularly in tense situations. Again, he credits the ethos of collaborative leadership that had been embedded in him during his time in uniform. 'People who are well trained to do their jobs do not require me to tell them how to do their work once they get started. What they need is clarity about the mission and the objectives, together with any support— material or moral—I can give them to help them perform their part of the task. *That* was my job as their leader.'

Mark Scott is a former managing director and editor in chief of the ABC, and is now the Secretary of the Department of Education in NSW. Scott worked with and was mentored by Graham when both were at Fairfax. 'Some might say he backed his team to a fault, and was too slow to move them if they were not always up to the task,' he remembers, 'but I saw the full picture.' Scott can cite many instances in which Graham's encouragement of his people in times of pressure had been a major factor in the team's success.

Somewhat belatedly, this concept is now being researched by scholars, under the label of 'servant leadership'. Its principles are based on the premise that leaders who are best able to motivate followers are those who focus less on satisfying their own needs and more on providing support for others. Servant leadership emphasises the business utility of the leader-as-catalyst mode, showing evidence of enhanced customer satisfaction, team cohesion and employee commitment.

How to stop ego getting in the way

Having a strong leadership ethos—particularly when it is expressed simply as mission-team-me—also helps to combat the 'ego conflict' that can arise when one is in a position of authority. Your head might tell you one thing ('It makes good sense to share the process') but often your heart and your ego tell you something quite different ('Hang on—*I'm* supposed to be the leader here—*I'm* supposed to be running things').

For leaders who have been assailed by such thoughts, the mission-team-me motto serves as an implicit reminder that the leader's ego is of small import compared to the goal, task and team capability. If others get the credit for a task well done and the process strengthens the team members, any minor bruising of the team leader's ego will have been a small price to pay.

In any case, team building is a leader's responsibility. Echoing Brigadier Roger Noble's earlier sentiments, former officer and now executive coach Russell Linwood notes that 'they may have been "soldiers" today but many of them [are] going to be the junior leaders of tomorrow. And if I didn't play my part in building their commitment and confidence, that tomorrow will be shaky'.

Lieutenant Colonel Charlie, a logistics specialist and former battalion commander, points to another advantage. In her earlier career days, especially 'as a woman in a very masculine culture', she worried that her willingness to take advice from subordinate leaders might make her seem indecisive and 'wavering or soft'. But she has long since shrugged off such concerns, and now feels that being true to herself makes her more flexible. This, she is certain, makes her a better leader because 'I don't have that ego tie-in that I see many people struggling with'. Her role model was one of her early bosses. 'It was fantastic working for her, because she was so easy to read. Passionate about what our team was doing, showed you what she was thinking, and would always argue on the basis of what she thought was right, not what would be good for her as an individual.'

Charlie's views are consistent with those of another of her senior colleagues. For Brigadier Delta, one of the most consistent threads linking every good leader with whom she has worked is that they achieved things through other people and genuinely saw people as their key asset. 'People do the work, and how you deal with and manage them is crucial,' she says, particularly when the task requires people to lift their performance beyond expectations.

'If people don't feel that strong sense of loyalty to you, they might happily and diligently work for you from 9 to 5; but then they will go home regardless.'

Onwards

A strong sense of who you are and what you value are key moral assets for maintaining focus and resolve in circumstances in which others might waver.

The Australian military ethos emphasises duty, responsibility and the imperative of working through, and looking after, the team. It is a particular way of thinking about oneself that sustains the concentration and psychological stamina needed for remaining focused and resilient in challenging situations. It was this thinking that Gerard Windsor detected in the behaviour of his friend Mark Maloney, and that embedded the values and priorities that were so important in the subsequent careers of the hundreds of young men who were trained as junior officers in the late 1960s and early '70s.

For both organisations and individuals, the guidance of such an ethos may well be one of the main differences between being 'good' and being 'great'.

5

THE 3RS OF LEADERSHIP
An overview

The standard you walk by is the standard you accept.

Lieutenant General David Morrison, AO,
citing an old military leadership dictum

Leadership is not about extolling the 'special stuff'
that sets some apart from others and projects them
into positions of power and influence but rather
about how leaders and followers come to see each
other as part of a common team.

Alexander Haslam, Stephen Reicher and Michael
Platow, The New Psychology of Leadership, 2011

Leading from the saddle

A recent news story provides a new angle on the public perception of military leadership.

It tells how a 'highly decorated former soldier who had led soldiers in Iraq' was exercising some influence in one of Australia's most notorious bikie gangs and was now driving recruitment for its latest branch.

The authorities' grudging respect for this ex-military leader is reflected in the comments of police and criminologists. A police source spoke of how this 'very capable' soldier was 'the perfect recruit for a gang like this', and how he had been 'very effective in restructuring the Bandidos'. A former inspector and now criminologist could understand why such gangs were keen to recruit former military leaders. 'If you're going to put someone in control of your group, who better than someone who's come from a command and control environment in the armed forces? They'll have a skill set that you would find almost irreplaceable.'

Despite the experience of the police in these matters, one can't help wondering if they misread the reasons for this former soldier's success with the bikies. Was it really because of his 'command and control' (and thus supposedly top-down) style? Or was it because of his ability to build teamwork and followership?

We will return to those questions at the end of this chapter. By that stage, you will have a clearer idea about the core leadership style used by former and current Army officers and soldiers, and why it is so effective in a range of contexts.

The '3Rs' of leadership

This chapter introduces a model that captures the essence of the captain-coach style that was introduced in Chapter 2. It is built around three main types of leadership activities: Representing, Relating and Running the team (see Table 5.1).

The 3Rs model evolved from a career's worth of experience, observation and research, which came to fruition and was 'stress-tested' in Marysville after the Black Saturday bushfires in 2009.

The model is built around a well-established principle: the most effective leaders are those who connect with followers' hearts as well as their heads; who do so by demonstrating their ability to bring about outcomes that are both practical and beneficial; who achieve goals in ways that also enhance followers' belief in themselves as individuals and as a team; and who leave their teams in good shape when they eventually move on.

The best leaders do all this by:

- **Representing** the behaviours, attributes and values that a team expects to see in its leader;
- **Relating** to members in order to make them believe in themselves, both as individuals and as a team; and
- **Running the team** so as to make working with that leader intrinsically rewarding as well as productive.

Each of these is represented in Table 5.1 by two main activities, with two examples of each. These dozen behaviours broadly encompass what is now recognised as 'best practice'.

Table 5.1: Building followership by practising the 3Rs of leadership

		Component elements	Examples of relevant behaviours
Representing: The role model	*Personify what the team stands for and expects to see in its leader*	Lead by example	• Display a sense of professionalism, proficiency, character, integrity and enthusiasm. • Set an example of doing the 'right thing' in terms of ethics and in going beyond self-interest for the good of the group.
		Give direction and meaning	• Frame organisational-level goals and issues in terms of what matters to the team. • Set clear short-term objectives that help members see their place in the bigger picture.
Relating: The supportive people manager	*Build self-belief and team spirit*	Treat members as valued colleagues	• Get out and about to talk face-to-face and share team activities. • Coach and counsel members individually and collectively.
		Develop individual and group identity	• Express enthusiasm for the team and its members, and provide special recognition when people do exceptional work. • Talk about 'we'/'us' rather than 'I'/'you', and share the credit for achievement.

		Component elements	Examples of relevant behaviours
Running the team: The engaging catalyst	*Make working with you intrinsically rewarding as well as productive*	Use team activities to build skills and work engagement	• Allocate clear responsibilities for achieving targets, and give people the 'elbow room' and the resources they need to get on with it. • Keep the team informed on individual and group progress.
		Encourage open-mindedness and a spirit of continuous improvement	• Encourage differing perspectives and fresh ways to tackle issues and challenges. • Conduct collaborative after-activity reviews and similar processes to learn and improve, both individually and collectively.

You will of course need to find your own ways of performing these, depending on your context. However, the next three chapters contain many examples, military and civilian, of ways in which this has been successfully done. (Consistent with the principle enunciated in the opening chapter, these examples concentrate on the positive only.)

The 3Rs model is simple and comprehensive. You can use it as a mental 'app' for planning your approach, guiding day-to-day behaviour, reflecting and self-critiquing, analysing and learning from others' behaviour, coaching and mentoring, and setting yourself up for success in a host of other ways.

Don't be misled by the focus on three ostensibly distinctive domains. In reality the process of leading involves a seamless and interrelated set of activities that are often difficult to separate. So stay alert for ways in which activities that are primarily associated with, say, Representing can be also relevant to Relating and Running the team, and vice versa. And also look for the ways in which many of these activities—even if they seem comparatively minor—reinforce each other and, by doing so, deliver a '1+1+1 = 4' effect.

Representing: The role model

To lead us, we look for someone who is worth following. We look for someone with the competence, character and integrity to deal with *our* problems and to give direction and meaning to what *we* do. We look for someone who is a worthy representative of what *we* stand for: someone we can identify with and believe in.

Representing is arguably the most important of the 3Rs. It's the price of entry: people are most likely to follow you if they believe you can deliver outcomes that matter to them and, conversely, they won't trust you if they have doubts in this respect. Moreover, superior competence in this domain can (at least partly) compensate for deficiencies in the other two Rs.

Don't, however, take this as a licence to be casual about dealing with people and team issues. As professionally competent as you might be, you will be even more effective if you pay appropriate attention to the full range of leadership behaviours.

Chapter 6 discusses Representing further, including many examples of its various aspects.

Relating: The supportive people manager

To lead us, a leader must relate to us in ways that make us feel as if our efforts matter.

Your willingness as a leader to do this is the best way to demonstrate how much you value your group members and their contribution. Treating them as if their efforts matter will boost their belief in themselves and in their team. Such feelings matter—a lot—in tight situations or in circumstances where people need to dig deep to meet a challenge.

We have already demonstrated the importance that Australians place on leaders who look out for the team and its members. Such a norm is quite at odds with the stereotypic 'tough guy' who supposedly earns obedience by heroic authority and has little tolerance for others' weaknesses.

Relating also helps to reinforce your representativeness, by demonstrating your human 'I'm-just-like-you' side.

You do all this not to 'be their friend' but to help them feel positively about themselves, the team and you. You should not hesitate to be firm and, if necessary, stern about adherence to standards. (This important point is made more than once in what follows.)

Chapter 7 discusses Relating further, including many examples of its various aspects.

Running the team: The engaging catalyst

To lead us, a leader must run the team in ways that give our activities intrinsic meaning and knit 'us' together as a cohesive entity.

Running the team is the 'sleeper' component of the 3Rs model. Most leaders would be able to nominate the activities associated with Representing and Relating as being important to the leadership process, but many will have given little thought to how team management can be enormously useful beyond simply coordinating and executing tasks.

What you do in this regard should consolidate all your other leadership activities. Good leaders use the team process to engage the spirit, strengthen self-belief, build a sense of common identity and cement a collective sense of agency ('*we* can do it'). They act as catalysts to help us perform and to simultaneously derive meaning and intrinsic reward from our work. All this makes working with them satisfying as well as productive. (Recall the NCO quoted in Chapter 3 who noted that one of the benefits of good leadership is that the team 'looked forward to coming to work each day'.)

Among the many benefits of doing so are that the team gets its work done in ways that enhance its capacity to do even better next time. More than that, such a style will make that leader seem more like 'one of *us*', again strengthening the sense of familiarity and common interest that team members will feel in working with that leader.

Such an approach to running a team is even more significant in the light of the Australian Army's inherent asset of independently minded people at all levels. As Sir John Monash said in one of the quotations that led Chapter 2, independent-mindedness is the 'best and not the worst foundation' on which to build team effectiveness. An inclusive and engaging approach to team management brings a host of benefits, not least of which is to allow the leader to focus on bigger-picture issues.

Incidentally, the tendency by Australian soldiers to question orders does not translate into rebelliousness or even insubordination.

It simply means that they will be independently minded even when, at least in the short term, they accept the need for compliance.

Chapter 8 discusses Running the team further, including many examples of its various aspects.

Multiplier effects

The various practices involved in the 3Rs have both multiplier and multiple effects. The more you as a leader are aware of these, the more likely you are to establish and sustain effective processes.

As a set of practices, the 3Rs tap into the full set of human needs. It provides a sense of security of being led by someone with authority and competence; it builds the satisfaction of social connection with the leader, with others in the group and with the larger entity to which that group belongs; it lifts self-confidence and self-esteem as a result of being treated as a respected colleague by a trusted leader; and establishes the self-actualisation and growth that come from doing good work in good company.

The performance effects of such an approach are tellingly illustrated in a recent leadership experiment conducted in the Israel Defense Force (IDF). Platoon commanders involved in recruit training were randomly allocated to one of two groups. Those in the 'experimental' group were given 3Rs-type leadership instruction; those in the control group received no special preparation. All platoon teams then spent several months training a series of recruit courses in basic soldiering. At the end of each such course, the performance of the various recruit squads was measured by standard tests in weapon handling, speed over an obstacle course, physical fitness, performance in minor tactics and written tests of military knowledge. These showed not only that the platoons trained by those in the experimental group performed better on most of the relevant measures but, equally importantly, that their NCOs had gained in self-confidence and team identification, and were more likely to both think independently and put above-average effort into their duties.

Research into such leader–follower processes has recently been given new life by the application of neuroscience. For example, a number of studies have shown that 3Rs-type leadership triggers the release of neurochemicals such as oxytocin (the so-called 'bonding molecule'), serotonin ('confidence') and adrenaline ('energy'). The stimulating effects on brain functioning and mood of these neuro-chemicals amplify the conscious/rational reactions to being well led, thus helping to make what 'makes sense' also be what 'feels good'.

Moreover, this double reinforcement effect often occurs within leaders themselves. As they see evidence of improved followership, they tend to experience the same kinds of neurological stimuli, thus making it more likely that they will continue to behave in such ways.

Leaders who can analyse their own behaviour accurately, and who can thus discern their influence on improved followership, will be those who will go from strength to strength. Conversely, those who can't make the connection will be less likely or able to perpet-uate such practices—to their detriment as well as to the detriment of the team.

'Command and control'—or just sound leadership?

Let's return to the case study of the former Army leader who led a chapter of a motorcycle gang. While the authorities attributed his lead-ership success to the 'similar command and control' cultures in each of the two institutions, there is a simpler and more practical explanation. It relates to leadership style but not in the way those authorities meant.

Most obviously, our former soldier would have earned respect and inherent authority by his demonstration of competence and character. Even his directive style may have been what the Bandidos expected and wanted, being what their situation often required. He would probably have reinforced this by forging strong relationships with gang members, if only because he would have known the importance of doing so, thus boosting their self-confidence and sense of group identity. Finally, he would have run the team appropriately and engagingly, with clear communication, delegation and other processes that would have further strengthened the gang members' sense of agency, unity and cohesion.

Regardless of whether we approve of what the gang does, the principles of effective leadership still apply. Leaders earn authority and trust by Representing what the team stands for, Relating to team members in ways that make them feel positive about themselves, and Running the team so as to strengthen both its processes and the positive feelings that result from being in it.

Onwards

There's still a lot of discussion about 'natural leadership'. But it's a mirage; and the closer you get to it the more you realise that natural leadership is essentially a fiction. Leadership is a *process* that involves a certain state of mind, supported by hard work and skill. And, as we noted above, the more you know, the better you'll go.

The next three chapters explore the essence of what is involved.

6

REPRESENTING
The role model

The secret of his popularity lay in the fact that he
possessed that rare and indefinable quality which
entitled the man to be regarded in the diggers' eyes
as 'dinkum'.

An ex-soldier, calling himself a 'digger spokesman',
on Sir John Monash, Anzac Day, 1924

The right words can have a galvanising effect,
generating enthusiasm, energy, momentum and
more, while the wrong ones can undermine the best
intentions and kill initiative on the spot, stone dead.

Stephen Denning, The Secret Language
of Leadership, 2007

Lifting our game

To lead us, leaders must represent 'us'. In conditions of uncertainty or risk, we look for someone with the competence, character and integrity to deal with *our* problems and to give direction and meaning to what *we* do. We look for someone who is a worthy representative of what *we* stand for: someone we can identify with and believe in. The Representing dimensions of the 3Rs model are replicated in Table 6.1.

Major Echo deployed to the Middle East to head up an established movement-control agency for Australian and local allied forces. Its various elements were dispersed across different areas and functions, and Echo knew that it was vital for the agency's various activities to be aligned around a guiding vision and clear set of priorities. Her first task was to sit down with her operations officer to examine her predecessor's report. She quickly saw that the agency had been operating in 'survival mode', getting by with what were essentially short-term priorities without any long-term plan to guide the process. She also discerned that the NCOs at the front line of the agency's activities would have a very good sense of what the agency's priorities should be. Because the 24/7 nature of the agency's activities prevented her assembling these NCOs for even a few hours' brainstorming and discussion, she asked them to email her about 'the top three issues keeping you up at night'.

Then Echo sat down with her operations officer to consolidate a list of key objectives and activities. They developed a vision—a blueprint—that proposed a number of changes to the unit's existing processes. This was disseminated to her immediate subordinates for comment, after which she telephoned each one to discuss how the vision would affect them, particularly in terms of what they could do to make it happen. She consolidated all this by making frequent visits to the various outposts, where she focused on what each could contribute to improved overall agency performance. Even though this would involve extra work for most of her subordinates, any reluctance they might have had on that front was quickly dispelled by Echo's enthusiasm, quiet confidence and evident professional expertise and understanding.

In Chapter 2's summary of the leadership behaviours that mattered to NCOs, the two themes mentioned most frequently were professionalism ('knowing their stuff', 'making the right decisions', 'focusing attention on things that matter', 'communicating their

Table 6.1: Building followership by Representing what the group stands for

		Component elements	Examples of relevant behaviours
Representing: The role model	*Personify what the team stands for and expects to see in its leader*	Lead by example	• Display a sense of professionalism, proficiency, character, integrity and enthusiasm. • Set an example of doing the 'right thing' in terms of ethics and in going beyond self-interest for the good of the group.
		Give direction and meaning	• Frame organisational-level goals and issues in terms of what matters to the team. • Set clear short-term objectives that help members see their place in the bigger picture.

intentions through language that makes sense to those at our level') and team and people focus ('rolling up their sleeves and joining in', 'spending time coaching and mentoring').

This chapter focuses on the first of these themes, and on what leaders should do to demonstrate that they 'have what it takes' in terms of leadership.

Lead by example

Display a sense of professionalism, proficiency, character, integrity and resolve

Professionalism, proficiency, character and integrity are core to leading by example.

From their earliest career stages, military leaders, are coached and tested in the fundamentals of problem-solving, decision-making and communications. They are taught 'the military appreciation process', analysing problems and making decisions in ways that systematically take into account all relevant factors, beginning with selecting the 'right' thing to do.

The military appreciation process balances decisiveness with deliberation. Indeed, one of the first factors to be considered is the time available for the analytical process itself. A dictum in military thinking is to allow adequate time for deciding just *what* it is you want to achieve before you rush into *how* to do so. It is all too easy to settle instinctively on a particular goal because of familiarity, habit or panic, and other impediments to systematic thought. A key rule of thumb: don't rush into the first apparently obvious option, so that if you have, say, 30 minutes to come up with a plan, spend the first ten deciding on your goal.

Terry Earle is one of many former national servicemen who subsequently made extensive use of this process. Four decades on, with a successful career in banking, management consultancy and small business behind him, he credits part of his success to the problem-solving skills he learned as a junior officer. 'Even nowadays, I rarely face a problem where I do not explore its nuances and options thoroughly,' says Earle. He tries 'to stick to the principle of thoroughly examining the nature of the problem in the first place, before I start exploring options'. It has helped him to detect innovative 'left field' solutions on many occasions.

Another advocate is Rob Senior, who served as an Army logistician before going on to a successful career in property planning and development. He believes that the military appreciation process helped him avoid many of the mistakes he saw being made by his civilian counterparts. He still remembers those 'well proven steps', and recommends that they 'should be shared and discussed with those involved, both so that they feel a sense of inclusion and so that you do not miss anything important'. And Graham Hiley, a former national serviceman and now a justice of the Northern Territory Supreme Court, still uses the approach in what he calls 'contemporaneous activity'. As the senior counsel in charge of teams of lawyers conducting big cases, he and his colleagues begin by drawing up a flexible plan that can be adapted as circumstances unfold, 'drawing on the organisational and leadership skills that I learned in officer training'.

Conveying a sense of positivity is important. Chris Brown was a junior officer in a Darwin-based signals squadron, commanded by Captain Peter Kerntke. Kerntke faced a particular challenge in the relief effort following Cyclone Tracy in 1974, when the squadron was tasked with restoring and maintaining communications to the highest possible level. With many soldiers' families based in Darwin, the troops found it hard to keep their thoughts focused on their work but, to Kerntke, 'this was the same as war'. Although they were all tired, Kerntke 'kept his cool and led from the front and helped us to keep our heads and spirits up and get the job done'. He was the kind of leader 'who did not need to remind you to do your best'.

Positivity is infectious. The dullest work can be enlivened by a leader's spark and good humour. Bob Slater left regular service as a lieutenant colonel, then rose to brigadier in the Army Reserve while working as a civil engineer and a CEO in the aged-care industry. He is active in Rotary, and fellow Rotarians see him as someone who never loses his composure or focus and who always treats disappointments as opportunities. This is notable in the way he encourages others to keep trying, and uses his wide range of networks to get around obstacles and open up opportunities. 'With Bob at the helm,' says one, 'I always felt a strong sense of purpose and confidence that we would achieve our goals.'

Russell Linwood took a similar approach to his post-Army role as the chief trainer of the Queensland ambulance service. From the start, he made every effort to get out and about to familiarise himself with its members and their work. It helped him become familiar with the organisation and its members, and boosted their respect for him. 'I didn't have to do it too many times for the word to spread that I was keen to learn about them and their work: that "he is a boss but acts like one of us",' he says. He would typically arrive at an ambulance station, introduce himself and request that he ride with them on their shift. 'I'll fit in to your operational process, you just tell me what to do.' Linwood also drew on the vehicle-driving skills he had acquired during his military service, so it was a short step to being competency-tested for the Queensland ambulances. 'This meant that I could sometimes free up the ambos for their more specialist medical activities. I just fitted in and acted as a member of the team at all times. I pulled my rank once only, and that was to get rid of a television helicopter during a crash crisis.'

Demonstrating your expertise in both minor and significant ways can be useful. When Lieutenant Colonel Mick King was CO of Townsville's Combat Service Support Battalion, he advised his young officers to 'find something that you can be good at that your diggers can identify with'. King was talking about the basic professional tasks of a soldier, rather than the more specialist skills required of officers, such as communications and staff work. 'You probably think those specialist skills are pretty important,' King said to his junior officers, 'and they are. But that means nothing to a soldier. Your soldiers will be looking for the concrete: for the evidence of what *you* can do that is similar to what *they* can do.'

Peter Howes took a similar approach when he worked with rescue and emergency volunteers soon after leaving the Army. He 'eased into it' by joining their swimming club, using that initial bond 'to get deeper into their world, and to understand them and their duties better'. Although Howes knew that the operational procedures needed updating, he didn't rush into the process. 'It would have been risky to have just said, "I've examined your procedures and I've decided that this is the way we will do it." That would have fallen flat!' His approach allowed him to gradually build up his credibility before he launched a critical examination of long-standing practices.

Another way of confirming your proficiency is in your policy on poor performance. An individual's performance won't always be satisfactory and sometimes this is not due to lack of effort. Showing patience towards such 'failures' and readily and constructively dealing with underperformance helps those team members to lift their game, as well as sending an important message to their peers.

Leading by example usually entails looking the part. Taking some trouble over how you dress denotes a level of respect for your colleagues and sends a subtle signal about how seriously you take your role as their leader. Professor John McCallum was one former national serviceman who took the obligations of dress standards into his civilian career. Presenting himself as a leader requires looking the part, 'so I dress for the role'.

Set an example of doing the 'right thing'

While your professional ability is important, you should not neglect the moral dimension. Your demonstration of character and integrity, even in small matters, is often seen as evidence of how likely you are to do the right thing when it comes to bigger issues ('the standard you walk by is the standard you accept').

Moral authority can be established subtly but powerfully by putting in extra effort and making personal sacrifices for the group. Good military leaders share their soldiers' conditions in the field, do the rounds of the sentry posts at night, join their soldiers for strenuous activities such as physical training, place themselves last in the mess line, help prepare and serve the soldiers' meals on special occasions such as Christmas dinners, and commit to a multitude of minor support activities that demonstrate their sense of unity to those who are nominally their subordinates. (Recall the story in

Chapter 4 of business executive Peter Graham's support for his team as they worked together to overcome the challenges of the union blockade of the new Fairfax printing plant at Tullamarine.)

As one experienced infantry NCO put it, 'When the soldiers are out there marching with their packs, those leaders would be beside them, marching with the same load. "If he can keep going when things are tough," you'd think to yourself, "I can as well." It matters!'

The ethic that underpins such choices is partly expressed by the military's principal that 'officers eat last'. Because soldiers know that their officers could take precedence in the distribution of rations if they wanted to—as well as in transport arrangements, accommodation and the like—the practice of standing aside while the soldiers' needs are met is seen as an indicator of commitment to the interests of the team, and that such a person is likely to 'do the right thing' in more challenging situations.

Retired Major General Mike Keating has a dictum that sums this up: leaders at every level must be prepared to give more than they receive, contribute without expectation of recompense, and put others' needs before theirs. And the converse applies. For example, it's unlikely that an officer I knew, nicknamed 'Dogdog' by his troops because he was always first in the mess line with his tongue metaphorically hanging out, would have been trusted very deeply by those soldiers.

Your team's trust in you will also be strengthened by your ethical consistency, in small as well as significant matters. What you do (as opposed to what you say) should leave as little ambiguity as possible about what is acceptable and what is not. This helps to reassure your team that you will be equally principled about things behind the scenes.

Patrick Gowans is a former senior officer who pursued a business career after his military service. One of his junior colleagues, Milly Yeo, remembers an incident that, although minor, has stayed with her as a telling example of principled behaviour. It concerned the board that Gowans chaired and to which she was secretary. The external auditor had requested the minutes of one of the meetings in which, coincidentally, the board had been highly critical of that auditor. Given that those remarks were recorded in the minutes, some board members suggested that the offending paragraph should be removed, even though all knew that this would have been illegal. However, when Gowans declared without hesitation that the minutes would remain intact without any editing, the matter was 'resolved without further discussion'. It was 'just a little thing', Millie recalls, but it meant a lot to those who were involved.

Former infantry battalion commander John Salter is remembered fondly by those who served with him. One of his company commanders, Bruce Scott, recalls him as 'a soldier's leader: a warrior'. A particular incident revealed much about Salter's style. It was after an unofficial battalion party in a nearby derelict warehouse—the 'piss-up of all piss-ups', as Scott put it—when the soldiers got 'very drunk and destroyed the place'. Salter assembled his soldiers, dressed them down and demanded that the organisers step forward. Because they respected him, they responded promptly. Salter then told them to 'take off your slouch hats and take them around the ranks: you are all going to pay for the damage'. Scott still marvels at 'the cleverness of it all'. It was not only the right thing to do, but also served to assuage any natural remorse that the soldiers might have been feeling after their spree. This approach lifted both morale and Salter's status to even higher levels. It was one of many comparatively small actions by which Salter embedded high standards in the unit and its members, so that when the battalion deployed for counter-insurgency operations in Somalia two or three years later (a case we looked at in Chapter 2), it performed 'very well', thanks in large part to Salter's legacy, as reported by Brigadier Chris Appleton, another of Salter's officers at the time.

Give direction and meaning

Frame organisational-level goals and issues in terms of what matters to the team

People expect a leader to provide direction and meaning, and to show them where they are going and why they are going there. This helps them to align their activities to the overall plan and strengthens their commitment to it.

Recall the example in Chapter 1 of Major General John Cantwell addressing the citizens of Marysville a few days after the devastating bushfires. Although they might have benefited from being told about the broader recovery strategy, Cantwell correctly anticipated their needs as being more immediate. So he focused on the short-term practicalities, reassuring the citizens while he informed them.

Beyond the short term imperatives of emergency management, however, there are great benefits in keeping people informed of your broader priorities. You should express these in ways that are meaningful and matter to them. An example is the approach the Marysville Community Golf & Bowls Club committee and I took in the weeks that followed the John Cantwell case above, as the club addressed its recovery challenges. We decided that our priority would be the first 9 holes of the golf course. The reason was much broader than simply to help members recommence their regular golfing routine. More deeply and strategically, the club needed to play its part in attracting tourists back into the district. As one of the very few viable businesses operating in the town in those early months, it was essential that the club be used to strategic advantage. The committee and I took pains to explain this to our members, and many appreciated this as an additional incentive to put in extra time on course repair work. I also spoke of this goal whenever I was talking to the community at large and to the many corporate entities and government agencies who were lining up to give support. This added to the legitimacy of what the club was asking of its many sponsors, and also gradually embedded the notion of the broader agenda in the minds of club members, thereby helping us to reach for goals that would have been completely unattainable in normal circumstances.

Set short-term objectives that help members see their place in the bigger picture

One of the ways in which we find meaning in our work is by believing that what we do matters. A leader can do this by showing team members their part in the bigger picture, however mundane it might seem to others. We saw a good example of this earlier in the chapter in the way that Major Echo worked to lift the performance of her unit in the Middle East, ensuring that each of her subordinate team leaders understood what they needed to do within the overall plan and how it would affect them.

Good communication can't be taken for granted. Wayne Jackson served in the Army for more than two decades and 'never ceased to be both amused and bemused' by how easy it was for an instruction given at a higher level to be corrupted by the time it reached the bottom. It was even worse when he went into business. Knowing the importance of clear and reliable communication, Jackson impressed on his subordinate managers the need to get accurate messages to the end of the communication chain, regardless of the time and effort required. He used a technique that military leaders call 'back briefing', by which a leader gives an instruction and then requires the recipient to repeat that instruction in his/her own words, thus confirming whether the recipient's interpretation is consistent with the leader's intended meaning. During his frequent visits to the operational levels of his business, Jackson would check on the extent to which this was happening by asking the frontline employees to give him their understanding of those messages. During these visits, he also ensured that each team had its own objectives and plan by requiring each local leader to tell him what these were, without reference to notes.

Jackson recalls that his biggest leadership challenge as a businessman was a task that involved integrating sets of specialist elements into a single entity. The challenge was to shake off previous modes of thinking, and to accept and commit to different approaches. He used to speak about this to everyone in the organisation, either face-to-face or in small groups. 'I would eyeball them, talk one-on-one, take questions. And for at least one afternoon each week, I would cement this with "management by walking around", as Peters and Waterman had called it.'

A wise leader takes every communication situation as an opportunity to influence and inform. And those who aspire to lead in the pragmatic, no-nonsense Australian context should be direct and engaging as well as comprehensive.

The Army has long drilled its leaders in the use of a basic communication protocol known as SMEAC (Situation, Mission, Execution,

Administration and Logistics, Command and Communications—explained in Appendix 2). The process is used for formulating and delivering orders in field settings, when leaders must communicate effectively despite time pressures and physical risk or danger. The protocol is based on two fundamental principles: it ensures you cover all the important points, regardless of any distractions; and that understanding the rationale for a plan can be important in motivating people. As Peter Graham remarks, 'it is very difficult to get serious buy-in from intelligent people if they do not have a clear understanding of the bigger picture'.

Thus the SMEAC protocol requires a leader to begin by placing the intended task in context, before going on to specifying the team's mission and how it will be done. This ensures that everyone understands the 'why' before they are told the 'what'.

It's a deceptively simple process. Such is its power and logic, however, that it was often singled out by many national service officers as among the most valuable takeaways from their short two years in uniform.

For example, Gordon Alexander, who subsequently made a career in communications and marketing, is one of them. He quickly grasped how the messaging process could be used as a way of engaging with people as well as for passing on information. The way that you communicate can and should 'show that you are interested, enthusiastic, empathetic and concerned for them', he says. He urges leaders to 'use simple, direct words; use active verbs; begin with a story that personifies the issues at hand; and show how that issue will be affected by what you are proposing'. He found that SMEAC is ideally suited for this purpose 'because its structure ensures that you will always cover the relevant issues'.

Alexander wasn't the only one. Generoso Calonge, a graduate of the Australian Officer Cadet School (OCS) who went on to military and public service in the Philippines, regards SMEAC as 'the one thing from OCS that remains with me to this day'. Jeff Kennett credits SMEAC as having helped him develop his renowned notes-free communication style. Among SMEAC's many advantages, he says, is that it 'helps you to avoid sermons and to focus on eye contact; and teaches you that what matters is the quality of what you say, not the length'. Peter Graham is another who still makes use of SMEAC, in an adaptation that he calls 'the Leadership Conversation'. He has long used this as the basis for his interaction with people and teams for whom he has been responsible, in the form of three key questions: 'What should I do? How will I know it is done? What then do you need?' If people are to be 'truly effective in their roles', Graham emphasises, it is 'critical' to explore such questions.

The utility of SMEAC as a communications protocol is an important reminder that you don't have to be gifted in order to be effective as a leader. Stephen Denning makes the point in one of the great books on the topic, *The Secret Language of Leadership*. While it is true that a leader's actions will eventually speak louder than his or her words, in the short run it is what that leader says—or doesn't say—that is important. Applying SMEAC is a way of ensuring coverage of the important points, thus freeing you up to concentrate on the delivery *method* as well as the *content*.

SMEAC will help you learn to speak on your feet, avoid hesitating or waffling, look people in the eyes when you are talking to them, put aside your notes and get away from the lectern. I made all those mistakes once, until I realised the more general utility of SMEAC, and began to draw on it for its much broader application beyond simply giving orders in the field. Thus began a long and grat-ifying journey to confidence and proficiency. You can and should do the same. It might be challenging at first but you'll be surprised at how easy it gets and how much more enjoyable the process of public speaking can become. Pretty soon it may well be one of your strengths.

Onwards

To lead us, leaders must represent 'us'. Representing—being a leader your team can believe in—requires you to lead by example and give meaning and direction to what your team does.

Under Major Echo's leadership the movement control agency's performance improved steadily. Explaining how it all happened some years later, Echo spoke of what she calls her 'integrative' approach: 'get in touch with those involved, tap their expertise, show them that their opinions and their actions matter, and keep their focus on the big picture'. When viewed through the prism of the 3Rs, however, we might well think that she was selling herself short. As a newcomer joining an experienced operational team in a predominantly masculine institution, Echo may have been tempted to leave things as they were. But her sense of duty forbade her from doing so, and she won the respect of her subordinates by her profes-sionalism, insight, competence and fair dinkum approach. Echo's behaviour encompassed the full constellation of Representing. She presented as a personification of what her team stood for and would have expected to see in its officers.

Representing is arguably the most important of the 3Rs. It's the price of entry: people simply will not trust you unless you demonstrate to them that you can be *for* them and *of* them, and can deliver the goods. If you don't measure up on that latter factor, you won't rate. But if you do measure up on all three, you are likely to earn your team's unstinting trust.

7

RELATING
The supportive people manager

If you asked the diggers about their commanders,
the biggest thing they will say is that they are good
at looking after us and standing up for us.

Chris Masters, Uncommon Soldier, *2012*

Paradoxically, in this highly masculine
environment filled with extreme danger, individual
consideration—the most stereotypically female
dimension of transformational leadership—appears
to be a key driver of a leader's repertoire as well
as success.

Kara Arnold, Catherine Loughlin and Megan Walsh,
Canadian researchers of contemporary practices in
the Canadian Armed Forces

Leadership by osmosis

Former national serviceman Noel Turnbull had always regarded himself as an unlikely soldier and an improbable officer. Indeed, one of his COs thought the same and accused him of having absorbed what little skill he had by osmosis rather than with effort and application. That remark must have planted a seed, because many years later Noel realised just how powerfully the Army's leadership training had influenced his attitudes and activities.

After a post-national service career in journalism and politics, he set up a PR company that ultimately became Australia's largest. For some time, he attributed the company's success to his and his colleagues' professional expertise. But a chance conversation one day with a friend from his Army days changed his mind. As his friend referenced his everyday managerial activities back to officer training, Noel realised just how deeply his military leadership experience had influenced almost everything he did in his company.

For example, Noel gained a fresh perspective on his habit of starting each day by walking around the office and talking to people about how they were and what they were doing. It was not some occasional nod to management-by-walking-around but a daily commitment, just as many years before he had started each day by walking around the battery lines to talk to the soldiers in his troop, to see how they were and whether they had any problems. Just as he had checked the gunners' mess at lunchtime to make sure everything was well, so he chased his desk-bound colleagues out for a lunchtime walk or sandwich in the interests of their welfare. Just as every day in the Army had been a day for training and learning, he used every meeting in the office as an opportunity to analyse what went well and what could be done better. Just as every activity in the Army was about building comradeship and a strong sense of the team, so every activity in the office, whether formal or informal, was used to create a sense of identity and pride in collective accomplishments. And just as every Army team wanted to be the best at what it did—better than everyone else in that or other regiments—so he encouraged the office team to think of itself as better than its competitors, even if it was just in an industry-wide Trivial Pursuits competition. When a flap was on in the office, Noel was available for advice or help. He was always willing to organise the late-night pizzas and coffees for those on a project, just as he had been trained to ensure his soldiers ate before he did. And when there were celebrations of success, it was always about 'us' rather than individuals or what he called 'the personal perpendicular pronoun'.

By osmosis Noel had recreated in a civilian office many of the features of an Australian Army unit: mutual respect, individual belief and competence, group identity, and an open-minded and egalitarian climate. In doing so, he was continuing a core practice that has been characteristic of the Australian military since its inception. Its continued relevance is shown in the quotation at the start of this chapter by journalist Chris Masters, together with the findings of my recent study of Army leadership, which found that the top indicator of 'good leadership' for both soldiers and officers was supportive people management.

The second quotation at the head of this chapter supports this empirically. It is from a Canadian study that investigated whether or not the traditional gender differences in leadership styles that had been observed in the private sector—with male managers generally more focused on tasks and females more focused on people—would be mirrored in the military. It found 'surprisingly' few discernible differences in gender-related leadership styles within the sample, not because women were leading in more masculine ways but rather the opposite: that is, male officers were leading in 'more feminine' (i.e., people-oriented) ways than their civilian counterparts. Those who were interviewed, regardless of gender, agreed that, without 'knowing your troops', a leader would be 'in serious trouble' in the extreme circumstances characteristic of military activities. Nonetheless, all officers were prepared to be highly directive when necessary, with many seeing the emphasis on an inclusive style as an investment in building trust they could draw upon in those rare but critical extreme situations.

Good people management doesn't happen overnight, and it is not achieved with generous benefits, big speeches or splashy occasions, but by consistent attention to many comparatively small things that all add up to something big.

Some of the main ways in which military leaders do this are shown in Table 7.1.

Treat members as valued fellow colleagues

Get out and about to talk face-to-face and share team activities

Leadership is a human activity and it demands a human touch. Those who feel valued by a leader walk with an extra spring in their step and take their work just that little bit more seriously. An important way in which leaders do this is by getting out to talk face-to-face and pitching in with the group's activities. The importance of doing this is illustrated by Chris Masters' earlier observation and by the frequency with which former national servicemen nominate 'looking after the diggers' as an important habit they learned during their military service. Its benefits were confirmed by my recent study, in which the NCOs interviewed spoke of how:

- 'you feel appreciated when your officer takes the trouble to get to know you and the other soldiers';
- 'it is a demonstration of a special effort—it is one thing to be competent in your job, but it takes extra effort to learn about your people'; and
- 'all these little things add up to bigger things. If you get the "one percenters" right, you start kicking goals'.

Table 7.1: Building followership by Relating constructively with group members

		Component elements	Examples of relevant behaviours
Relating: The supportive people manager	*Build self-belief and team spirit*	Treat members as valued colleagues	• Get out and about to talk face-to-face and share team activities. • Coach and counsel members individually and collectively.
		Develop individual and group identity	• Express enthusiasm for the team and its members, and provide special recognition when people do exceptional work. • Talk about 'we'/'us' rather than 'I'/'you', and share the credit for achievement.

The effect of being consistently fair dinkum in team relation-ships can be profound, particularly when you take this approach beyond simple everyday managerial obligations. Joining in, sharing the load and even just being on time and keeping your commit-ments—all these little things can add up to something big if you do them sincerely and consistently. As a leader, you need to show that you don't hold yourself as being better just because of your rank or position. As former Army officer David Pierce puts it: 'Subordi-nate to you but no less important.' Pierce proffers a related piece of advice mentioned by many others: don't send an email when you can make a phone call; and don't phone when you can talk face-to-face.

Good leaders recognise the importance of engaged listening. Former Army officer and now business executive Jim Clement sees it as one of the subtle but more important attributes of successful executive behaviour. 'The most effective executives I have worked for listened, consulted and then decided; the ineffective ones just decided.' It wasn't simply the act itself, but what it implied about the mindset. He should know: after twenty years of military service, Jim set up a business that grew from mowing the occasional domestic lawn to contracting his services to governments and major companies.

Similarly, former national serviceman Dick Whitaker, who served as an infantry officer before going on to a successful career in meteorology, recalls the most effective officers as being those who not only listened to what others had to say but also incorporated part of what they heard into their planning and decision-making. Not only did they thereby demonstrate respect but, because they were listening closely, they picked up many important subtleties about a situation that they might otherwise have missed.

A good leader establishes a routine to help this happen. For example, when he was a major commanding an artillery battery, former Vice Chief of the Defence Force Lieutenant General Des Mueller invited three or four junior soldiers in for a chat every day after lunch. Although it was his way of keeping in touch with them, he later heard on the grapevine that they saw this as a sign that their senior officers genuinely cared for them. Mueller was following a dictum espoused by infantry CO, Lieutenant Colonel (later Major General) Brian ('Hori') Howard who impressed on his junior officers that morning tea breaks were to be spent 'sharing a brew with the troops'. They were to use the opportunity to talk to soldiers, find out what they were thinking and what their problems were, and generally gain their confidence. Former battalion commander Lieutenant Colonel Mick King had a similar practice. Accompanied by his regimental sergeant major, he 'would just walk around and say g'day. I wanted my soldiers to feel that they could walk past my office, catch my eye and wave and say g'day. A couple of them subsequently told me how much they appreciated it.'

A busy manager needs to make time for this. Navy Warrant Officer Foxtrot recalls a boss who kept a big GOYA ['Get off Your Arse'] sign behind his desk. 'He would point over his shoulder with his thumb when talking about how to tackle a leadership issue to drum it into us—GOYA, GOYA. Forget your bloody in-tray. Get out there; interact with your people; find out what's happening and show them that they matter to you.'

It's important that the more senior people encourage their junior managers/leaders in this practice. Major Golf ruefully recalls the 'disconnect' that existed between him and his soldiers when he was a junior officer. The younger Golf not only lacked the confidence to engage with them but was also unlucky enough to have had some poor senior role models earlier in his career. Looking back, he sees this as a complicated mixture of narcissism and the desire to ape the British Army model: a model that 'was not and never will be appropriate in Australia'. He had seen getting out to engage with soldiers as a 'risk to my authority', but he now sees this perspective as an indication that 'I hadn't really become comfortable in my own skin with my responsibilities as an officer'. Having now 'seen the light', Golf makes officer–soldier connection one of the main points that he 'drums into' his junior officers.

Such practices have additional psychological effects that are subtle but profound. Perhaps most importantly, taking an interest in your people will be seen by them as a practical demonstration that you regard yourself as being 'one of the team'—one of 'them'. It enhances the sense of 'of us, with us, for us' that was emphasised in previous chapters.

Coach and counsel members individually and collectively

Every leader should spend time coaching and counselling. It is at the top of Navy Warrant Officer Artie Lavender's list of 'lessons learned' for the Navy's budding leaders. 'Team members often have talent and potential, and that needs to be brought forward and nurtured,' says Lavender, emphasising that a wise leader does this regardless of any immediate payoff.

One of Lavender's contemporaries relates an example of how this was done. Navy Warrant Officer Hotel has set up what she calls an 'influence network', comprising both senior and junior sailors. This allows as many voices as possible to be heard and, equally importantly, gives her junior people the chance to develop their leadership expertise. She 'takes a lot of trouble' to identify those with influence in their peer group and then concentrates on those key influencers. As part of the process, Hotel ran a leadership forum for senior sailors and then had each of them chair a similar forum for their junior sailors. This had a number of benefits. It helped those at her level to get messages around and about quickly and reliably; it enabled the more senior people to discuss the 'why' associated with certain decisions ('once you know *why*, you can identify what you need to change and develop, set targets and build towards them'); and, 'not least', the whole process served as an informal ongoing seminar of leadership for all concerned.

Amanda King remembers the longer-term effects of working with Patrick Gowans (whom we met in the previous chapter) in one of the businesses he ran after leaving the Army. 'He changed my life; he really did. He made me feel that I was a person worth listening to, and he encouraged me to push the boundaries of my life in all sorts of ways. Thanks to Patrick, I got myself to university and I applied for and got promotions. He even got me dating a better class of men!' She attributes working with Gowans as the main driver of her strong commitment to excellence.

Experienced military leaders stress the benefits of a constructive approach to coaching, as opposed to straight-out criticism. 'Let's examine what we can both do to help you do better' usually works better than 'You are not performing well and you must lift your game'. One officer spoke of how a former company commander didn't necessarily solve his problems but, 'by talking to [me] about them, gave me a sense that he was willing to do so if I wasn't able to do it [myself]. He fostered growth by challenging me to sort things out myself'.

It's important to appreciate the subtle but important difference between being supportive and being friendly. Former officers frequently speak of their application of the FFANF principles (Firm, Fair, Approachable but Not Friendly) in dealing with colleagues. Avoid having favourites; deal with everyone on the same concerned but objective basis; discipline people when necessary; and apply 'tough love' in coaching them to better performance levels. In short: be a supportive colleague, and often a 'mate' but never a 'Mate'.

This has long been standard practice in the Australian military. For example, renowned First Australian Imperial Force (1st AIF) World War I commander Pompey Elliott had a reputation as a tough disciplinarian but, as biographer Ross McMullen writes, his soldiers regarded him as being 'absolutely straight, and incapable of deviousness: you knew where you stood with Pompey'. They appreciated the way the CO took a personal interest in them as individuals, even though he had more than a thousand men under his command.

David Pierce affirms this aspect of an officer's style: 'You have overall responsibility so at times you must show a less friendly side when correcting mistakes and disciplining.' Experienced NCO Corporal India similarly advises young officers to avoid the trap of 'being too chummy with the lads'. Soldiers want to see their officer as 'their constant', India says, 'and that requires the officer to maintain a professional demeanour'.

Develop individual and group identity

Express enthusiasm for the team and its members

A sense of identity ('who I am') that is closely aligned to the work role is a powerful element in giving meaning to what people do and with whom they do it. An important way by which this can be developed is by treating individuals and the team as if their work really matters.

However mundane a task might be, the spirits and motivation of those involved can be lifted by the enthusiasm displayed by the team's leader.

Enthusiasm was a vital factor in the performance of an infantry platoon deployed to Timor-Leste as a regional Quick Reaction Force (QRF) in late 2001. It was more than a year after the 1999 intervention and the local environment had become so stable that there was little likelihood that the QRF would be called out. Although the task had to be done, the soldiers were beginning to see it as 'a waste of time'; and after weeks away from families and friends, for what seemed like no good reason, many platoons finished their deployment in low spirits. But young platoon commander Lieutenant Juliet was determined not to let this happen. 'You have two options,' he told his soldiers, 'You can sit around and feel bored and sorry for yourselves, or you can throw your efforts into doing something you can be proud of.' To keep his team on its toes, Juliet set up a tough program of physical fitness and riot-control training so intense that other groups in their camp expressed concern that the platoon was overdoing it. Far from being deterred, however, his soldiers became swept along by the process. Before long, the platoon was achieving response times of less than 60 seconds, compared to its predecessor's time of seven minutes. And although—as predicted—the platoon was not activated during its two-month deployment, it returned to Australia as a tight-knit and professional team with high morale.

Another example is that of Wing Commander Kilo, the CO of an operational squadron. Apart from his flying activities, he had a host of other duties to perform. Despite his busy schedule, however, he always made time to visit the squadron maintenance area, popping in two or three times each month and usually taking a few of his more junior aircrew with him to show those working in maintenance that the senior man's enthusiasm for them was widely shared. On each visit he would talk about a particular aspect of maintenance, express his appreciation for the way it was being done and commend his support crews' professionalism. It was a valuable reinforcement for those crews, and an equally valuable lesson in leadership for his junior officers.

Another former staff member of senior officer Patrick Gowans, Milly Yeo, recalls him as 'so passionate in his role that one couldn't help but share the passion'. Working with Gowans was a very productive learning process, because 'his door was always open, and his wealth of knowledge on any subject meant that there was never a time when he did not have an answer to my questions'.

Talk about 'we'/'us' rather than 'I'/'you', and share the credit for achievement

Language is a powerful way of creating a sense of group distinctiveness and pride.

Many former and currently serving military members spoke about the importance of providing special recognition for exceptional work. This not only reinforces such behaviour, thus making it more likely that it will occur again, but also signals to the team at large the nature of what a leader sees as important—including those many 'little things' that are not necessarily included in job specifications but are nonetheless valuable.

Naval Warrant Officer Lima is 'passionate' about playing her part in making the Navy's communication style more inclusive and representative of Australian society. 'We do the big things really easily,' she says, 'but it's the seemingly little things—whose combined effects are potentially huge—that are going to be the breakthrough.' She recalls one ship's captain who was particularly diligent in this regard. He would frequently come onto the PA system and commend the ship's company for an activity that had just been accomplished. Lima recounts one instance after the ship had provided assistance to a fishing boat that had been in trouble in a very heavy sea. Her captain spoke warmly of a small team of sailors who had played a particularly significant role in this action, but then concluded by stressing that this would not have been possible without the support of the whole ship's company. He spoke of how this cohesion and skill were the result of both training and working together, a process by which a group of sailors had become a 'crew'. It wasn't long, she reports, before the whole ship's company was feeling a sense of unity: the sense that 'we can do anything'.

Russell Linwood, an executive in the Queensland Ambulance Service, whom we met in a previous chapter, is another leader who is particularly diligent about recognising individual contributions. His colleague John Longhurst spoke of how Linwood 'always saw the best in you and focused on the positive: he would mention what I'd done well, point out opportunities for improvement, then close with a final word of commendation. It had a gradual but nonetheless enormously beneficial effect on leader-team and member-confidence. You would walk out of his office feeling inspired.'

Former national serviceman Warren Thatcher was also the beneficiary of such leadership behaviour. Thatcher recalls the 'especially powerful' effect when his company commander passed on praise from outsiders. 'He would emphasise that this was an indication of the respect that outsiders had of us as a team. That sense of "doing it well together": it's an enormously powerful reinforcer that gives benefits over and over again.' (Thatcher mentions another of his boss's useful habits: he would often make 'a quiet suggestion on how to do it better next time!')

It is useful in this respect to take advantage of any legacy associated with the organisation, so that team members can see what they do within the continuum of that organisation's history. Armoured Corps CO Duncan Hayward would invite members of regimental associations to visit his unit and interact with his troopers. 'Simply talking together was useful for both parties,' he says. 'It confirmed to the former members the importance of what the current crop did, and it reminded these serving soldiers that they had a legacy to live up to.'

A more light-hearted example concerns the artillery battery with which I served in Vietnam. The gun lines of the field batteries of the era were organised into two troops, each of three guns commanded by a junior officer. The two junior officers on the 104th Field Battery gun line were Wayne Kendall and Ernie Bryon. Wayne's soldiers called themselves 'Kendall's Koalas' and, consistent with an Australian joke of the time, their motto was 'Eats, roots and leaves'. In response, Ernie's troop began calling itself 'Bryon's Bears', with the motto 'Eats, roots and leaves and belts shit out of koalas'. Not surprisingly, this simply heightened the friendly rivalry between the two troops, with soldiers in each team often spurring each other on so as to 'not let those bloody Koalas [or Bears] beat us'.

Onwards

The motivational payoff of working on relationships is more powerful than most people realise. Being treated as a respected colleague by a respected leader is a powerful motivator. It is powerful because it boosts self-esteem and also subconsciously impels people to conform to such expectations; it enhances the value they place on particular kinds of activities and goals, and thus affects what they attend to and see and hear. And if they are also encouraged to think of themselves as those 'who can do it', they will be that much less likely to falter under pressure.

You will need to find time for it, but it will be worthwhile in the longer term. Defy the stereotypes that lurked behind the Canadian military study reviewed earlier; do what Noel Turnbull did and make it part of your daily routine. Like Noel, you might be surprised at just how beneficial it turns out to be for both you and your team.

The potential effects are brilliantly depicted in the opening minutes of the movie *Gladiator*. You might recall the scene. It is late autumn in the deep forests of northern Germany, and a Roman army is preparing for battle against their barbarian foes. The young general (played by Russell Crowe) rides up, tethers his horse and makes his way through the ranks of his legionnaires to a makeshift command post. As he does so, the soldiers turn towards him and salute, bow and in other ways acknowledge his presence. For a moment, their actions look like deference—the obligatory acknowledgement of formal authority by subordinates. But it quickly becomes obvious that something much more profound is happening, and that these people—the general on the one hand and the legionnaires on the other—care about and believe in themselves and in their team; and that they will fight to the death for each other. (Given the points made in Chapter 3 regarding the Australian approach to leadership, it was perhaps fitting that an Australasian played the Roman general in the movie. Crowe is equally convincing as the 'master and commander' of a Royal Naval ship in a film of the same name set in the Napoleonic era.)

If interpersonal relationships don't come easily to you—as is often the case with introverts or those who feel somewhat overawed by the ability and experience of those with whom they are dealing— it is perfectly okay to 'fake it till you make it'. Keep reminding yourself to behave in particular ways. Remind yourself to shut up and listen, to look that person in the eye, lean towards them, nod and ask affirming questions, and so on. Use the checklist in Table 7.1 as a prompter and a scoresheet.

Does this seem manipulative? Far from it. Relating to your people in these ways will not only make a substantial difference to their morale and effectiveness, but will also enhance your attention to what's going on and encourage people to open up to you, sharing information they might have kept to themselves had they sensed a lack of interest on your part. Conscious practise of this useful set of habits will, in time, become so much part of your own repertoire that it will come naturally.

And, by essentially the same reciprocal and neurochemical process that was discussed in the two previous chapters, the process is also likely to boost your own sense of satisfaction and fulfilment.

8

RUNNING THE TEAM
The engaging catalyst

I suspect that throughout history more good has
been done by good people acting well than by any
number of experts trying to predict and manipulate
outcomes, especially economic outcomes.

Hugh Mackay, social analyst, 2001

One of the Australian Army's greatest advantages
is the expectation that subordinates will question
their leaders' decisions and will make appropriate
suggestions. Creating this command culture is one
of the biggest challenges of an effective commander.

Major General Jim Molan, AO, DSC, September 2017

Reinforcing the leadership process by how you run the team

Lieutenant Colonel Mick King took command of his logistics support battalion in Townsville during the long gap between Vietnam and East Timor. Like other COs, King was keenly aware of the challenge of keeping his unit on its toes at a time when there were no external demands that could serve as natural focus points for engagement. And, like other COs, King was convinced that it was only by activity at battalion level and below that the Army could remain focused and relevant. So he determined to run his unit in ways that involved the widest possible engagement in contemporary soldiering.

King's command philosophy had three main themes: be ready, seize opportunities, be brilliant at the basics. In many ways, large and small, he made them part of everyday discourse in his unit. For example, when talking to his officers and soldiers, King would frequently refer to his themes by linking them to anecdotes of current and historical military leadership; he also included the three themes in the footer of the unit's PowerPoint slides template. He emphasised to all ranks that they were 'soldiers first', and that soldierly skills came before trade skills. 'When the call comes,' he would tell his soldiers, 'and it will, we will be ready to play our part.' All this was reinforced by a practice of 'do as I do'. He routinely attended morning physical training and range practices as well as other work and training activities to show his troops that the CO was just as prepared as they were (and thus implied—not so subtly—that all other leaders and unit members had a similar responsibility).

King continually worked on his officers' understanding of bigger-picture issues and on giving them a better idea of what they needed to do to support him and the whole unit. He encouraged them to take the initiative if and when they needed to, and to impress the same on their team members. 'Stick your hand up if you like to be identified with failure,' King would say to his officers. 'Well, that goes for your diggers as well. The best way you can motivate them is to help them feel that they are making a contribution to the best of their abilities.'

In the second year of his command, after the battalion won the brigade military skills trophy in a series of competitive events that were usually dominated by the brigade's combat units, King told his soldiers that the thing that made him proudest of the accomplishment was that 'we did it together'.

Although accounts of military leadership are often illustrated by examples of heroic and inspirational activities, real life for the vast majority of leaders and teams comprises many mundane work activities. But, with skilful leadership, these often add up to something significant.

Smart leaders give as much attention to the routine as they do to dealing with crises, running their teams in ways that not only get the work done today but also enhance those teams' capacity for even better performance tomorrow. By making the process part of the product, they gain a double benefit.

Of the many useful lessons for organisational leadership in the Lieutenant Colonel King case study, perhaps the most important one was the way that he drew his soldiers at all levels into the process. Somewhat like ex-Lieutenant Colonel Colin Toll in the Mount Blue Cow case study in Chapter 3, King challenged his team members at all levels to reach beyond the norm in what they did as individuals and together.

Both provide classic examples of ways of Running the team, the core elements of which are summarised in Table 8.1.

Table 8.1: Building followership by Running the team in ways that engage group members

		Component elements	Examples of relevant behaviours
Running the team: The engaging catalyst	*Make working with you intrinsically rewarding as well as productive*	Use team activities to build skills and work engagement	• Allocate clear responsibilities for achieving targets, and give people the 'elbow room' and the resources they need to get on with it. • Keep the team informed on individual and group progress.
		Encourage open-mindedness and a spirit of continuous improvement	• Encourage differing perspectives and fresh ways to tackle issues and challenges. • Conduct collaborative after-activity reviews and similar processes to learn and improve, both individually and collectively.

Using team activities to build engagement with the work itself

Allocate clear responsibilities for achieving targets, and allow people to get on with it

Part of your effectiveness as a leader will depend on the way you run your team's processes. In practical terms, this means giving team members appropriate autonomy (or, in colloquial terms, 'elbow room') and allowing them to use and build valued skills. People whose work includes those qualities tend to have high levels of commitment and engagement. Encouraging members to see their work in 'more-than-just-a-job' terms—that is, getting them to see their work as an integral part of the broader team effort—helps them to derive even more meaning from what they do. It all makes working with you satisfying and rewarding for its own sake.

If a team member has expertise in fixing things, for example, it is highly likely that he/she will take pleasure in the opportunity to fix things. Moreover, if you have a team member with significant expertise in fixing things and another with a lesser level of expertise, you can often meet the intrinsic needs of both by getting them to work as a mini-team. When the 'expert' coaches the 'novice', each is likely to gain from the experience. The effect is doubled if you later acknowledge their joint accomplishments in terms of their contribution to the larger group.

Delegation and sensible autonomy benefits everybody, says Duncan Hayward. When he was CO of the 1st Armoured Regiment, he motivated his young officers by allowing them to do their jobs and putting them in positions where they could make mistakes without too much risk. He would tell his young officers that 'lieutenants who don't make mistakes are not trying hard enough' (although he noted privately that 'if they made the same mistake more than once it did attract my attention!'). Hayward emphasises that any tendency towards a zero-tolerance mentality should be resisted, on the grounds that it would damage the Army's leadership-development culture.

Bruce Elliott is a former national serviceman who credits his military experience for his subsequent success in an academic career that culminated in his fifteen years as a head of school at the

University of Western Australia. Elliott acquired his expertise in sport science, exercise and health when, as a national service officer, he headed the Army's embryo physical education facility. All his staff were regular NCOs, and thus he also learned the habits of delegation and consultation that became an important part of his leadership style—giving his current subordinates a sense of engagement with the institution's goals and activities.

Don Ramsay made a successful career in mining after his national service. He often reflects on how his military experience taught him the importance of showing a 'genuine respect for the people working with and for me'. His approach was to ensure the lines of authority and accountability were clear and straightforward. People need to know what their job is and what they will be held accountable for, he says, and leaders need to continually encourage team members to look for innovative ways to improve routine processes. 'If the team is well trained and confident then all you need to do is ask and the job will get done. No need for the pistol. And in corporate life, it is even more important to ask the question in the right way, and then have the team want to do what needs to be done in the timeframe required.'

Jim Clement, whom we met in the previous chapter, used 'the fist within the velvet glove approach' in both his military and business careers. He would 'politely' ask that something be done, 'when we all knew that, as an officer or the boss (in later life), I had the power to order or demand'. Far from weakening your position, as some might think, Clement believes that the opposite is usually the case. He took the same approach in his business career—ensuring his workers were well trained, keeping his people in the picture, always being available for complaints or suggestions and challenging his immediate subordinates to do the same.

Of course, an individual's performance won't always be satisfactory; and while it is one thing to acknowledge good results, it is a different matter when someone's performance is poor, even when it is not due to lack of effort. As we saw in the previous chapter, showing patience towards such 'failures', as well as readily and constructively dealing with underperformance, helps those team members (even though they might not like it at that time) and also sends important messages to their fellows.

As noted earlier, an important principle that underpins the definition of leadership in Chapter 2 is that your leadership style should reflect both current realities and future situations that might be just around the corner. Consistent with the Canadian military study reported in the previous chapter, which showed that responsible leaders use the easy times to prepare for the tough ones, a number of current and former Australian service personnel also stress the importance of taking a longer view. For example, Miles Newman, a former military engineer who now runs a project management consultancy, 'found that people are much more amenable to directive leadership if you are consultative and inclusive most of the time. In times of crisis you can then say, "Do it now; I'll tell you why later."' This particularly applies when team members may not readily recognise a situation as being a 'crisis', and they will therefore 'have to take you on trust'. Thus, 'you have to spend a lot of time building trust and capability so that you can draw on it for when it matters'.

Such investment and foresight is evident in an incident I recall from my time in Vietnam, when I was an artillery forward observer with an infantry company that spent most of its time patrolling in the jungle. The incident in question happened late in the afternoon of another wearying day on a mission that had already lasted more than a fortnight. Most of this time had been spent in close and airless scrub during the dry season, and we were all knackered and ready to drop. Just before we got to the planned destination for the evening, company commander Major Bill Reynolds summoned the platoon commanders and their sergeants to a brief huddle. Reynolds announced that the usual drill for securing and occupying an overnight position was to be varied. The 'usual drill' was for each platoon to systematically occupy its assigned sector, then send out a small clearing patrol for a hundred metres or so. This was still to be done but, on this occasion, the platoon commanders and their sergeants would conduct the clearing patrols. While they were doing this, all the other members of the platoon could take fifteen or so minutes 'to flake—just this once'. The tactical risk, the company commander explained, was slight: if the clearing patrols did strike trouble, the rest of the company would instantly spring into action. Reynolds concluded by telling each platoon commander to give the order as if it was his own idea.

It must have been hard for those platoon commanders and their sergeants to find that extra effort, but of course they did. And the various payoffs would have been considerable. It demonstrated the seriousness with which Reynolds and his officers took their soldiers' welfare; it enhanced the regard in which they were held by their troops; it showed those soldiers that their leaders were willing and able to keep going beyond normal expectations; it boosted the platoon commanders' and sergeants' confidence in themselves and in their boss; and, not least, it served as a moral leadership master class that would stay with them—as it has for me—for decades.

One of the main techniques used by military organisations in running the team and making networked hierarchy work is the distinctive collaborative leadership process known as mission command.

Mission command requires leaders at all levels to task subordinate leaders by providing them with the information, resources and elbow room they need to tackle specific objectives semi-autonomously within an overall plan. Those subordinate leaders are then left to get on with their part of the operation, keeping the central leader informed on progress and issues as necessary, thus allowing that central leader to monitor and manage the broader picture. The practice goes back at least to the 2nd AIF in World War II and also the Australian contingent of the Commonwealth Brigade in Korea. In day-to-day operations in Vietnam in the 1960s and '70s, even privates often had significant responsibilities. A platoon forward scout, for example, was expected not only to deal with dangers that might unexpectedly emerge from the jungle during company-level sweep-and-search operations but also to assess the terrain for any potential dangers. As the person closest to the action (and, in close jungle, often the only one who could see what was ahead), the forward scout was usually empowered to make decisions for and act in the interests of the patrol. This private had to act as both an intelligence officer and a rifleman.

The routine practice of delegating to the frontline troops was one of the biggest surprises that Peter Graham recalls from his time in uniform. 'While I could understand the delegations that followed rank—company commander to platoon commander, platoon commander to section commander, and so on—it was the significant level of delegation to the very frontline that was the surprise. I quickly learned that this practice had been long tried and tested in pressure situations. And the high level of training and practising from private[s] . . . upwards helped to build confidence in both [the] leaders and [the] led.'

It was a principle that Graham went on to use throughout his business career. He regarded the time he spent training and testing the competence of those in every corporate team he headed as a 'terrific investment'. Not only was it 'more effective and more efficient than anything that I saw most of my colleagues doing but—more importantly—it was more than vindicated by the trust I earned from my team by showing that I trusted them'. And a not insignificant bonus was that these practices resulted in 'a far more enjoyable and interesting work situation for everybody, as well as giving them a strong sense of working together'.

Keep the team informed on individual and group progress

Part of the process of good team management is to inform people on progress. Keeping people in the picture serves several purposes, including reassuring them that the team is on track, spurring them on if it is not, and sharing the satisfaction of achieving milestones.

An example was seen in the Major Echo case study that launched Chapter 6. Echo and her senior colleagues worked together to introduce a number of changes to the workings of their movement-control centre in Afghanistan. She kept her subordinates appraised of overall agency performance, not so much to motivate them as to enable them to see and learn from the implications of both improvements and setbacks.

In a similar way, Amanda King, another colleague of Patrick Gowans (from previous chapters), spoke of how he always kept everybody informed about the big picture. 'Because Pat always had the overall goal in mind, he made us interested in it too. You knew exactly *why* you were working for him. He told us about how things were going, asked us for suggestions, and helped us see what was happening. It increased my level of engagement very much.'

Encouraging open-mindedness and a spirit of continuous improvement

Encourage differing perspectives and fresh ways of how to tackle issues

The final element of the 3Rs model is to encourage initiative, adaptability and innovation.

Work teams benefit by regularly searching for alternative approaches and innovations. Emphasising the importance of being innovative and staying alert for the unexpected is not only simply good management but also demonstrates to team members their value as contributors to the process. (Again, it is an example of how one action serves many outcomes.)

When Flight Lieutenant Mike was assigned to the Air Force's recruit-training unit, her CO took advantage of her experience and skills as a qualified business coach to improve overall unit performance. The CO had Mike develop a coaching action plan that could be gradually extended across the whole unit and then had her facilitate a series of 'Coaching 101' workshops aimed at fundamentally changing the ways in which instructors engaged with recruits. The success of these workshops encouraged Mike to suggest to her boss that she form and mentor a small group of 'coaching champions' to be the agents of change within the unit, and who could assist other instructors in solving problems, taking acceptable risks and being more agile in thought and action. Her program resulted in greater self-awareness, teamwork, communication and development of leadership skills among the instructional body at large.

Conduct collaborative after-activity reviews to learn and improve

Smart leaders use the team process itself to review and improve team functioning. The very act of reviewing what happened and how it might be improved next time helps to bring the team closer together and also taps the energy and enterprise of its members.

Peter Graham recalls his 'enormous luck' when he was a young national service officer serving under a company commander, Bob George, whose perspectives on performance at first struck him as unusual. George not only set high standards, but also showed 'real enthusiasm' for failures as well as successes. 'It may seem strange to say that he was "enthusiastic" about failure,' Graham says, 'and I don't mean to imply that he was happy with failing. What I mean is that he systematically examined openly and honestly what happened, particularly when it didn't work, in order to determine what should be done about it next time so that we could ensure it didn't happen again.' The company commander was open to all perspectives, whether or not it reflected well on his actions, because he saw this as the means of improving team and organisational performance.

We can imagine how this example of professional integrity was an enormously important learning experience for a young man who was still grappling with the conflicting requirements of wanting to make a good impression on the one hand, and doing the right thing on the other.

Gary Allan left the Army as a senior officer and is now an IT executive. He stresses that learning should be incorporated into routine activities whenever possible in order to improve collective capability. We have to 'replace ourselves' in due course, Allan points out, and creating a learning environment helps to make that process as seamless as possible. He adds that when you do give junior people a work assignment you should allow them to 'fail', as long as they learn from the experience (possibly with your assistance). The bonus for such an approach is that it demonstrates concern and commitment to the team, thus further solidifying the relationship and trust between leader and followers.

The Army has a standard but semi-formal process for conducting an After Action Review (AAR) to ensure that a team can learn while it is performing. This ensures that it doesn't have to wait for an official 'post-mortem' to figure out what went wrong and what went right.

An AAR is not needed for every incident and every outcome. Concentrate on those where improvement would be most valuable, or from which you can learn the most. Just as importantly, use the AAR process as a way of passing on lessons to other teams.

Table 8.2 sets out the basic design principles and the fundamental questions for an AAR.

Table 8.2: The AAR

AAR design principles	The five fundamental questions for an AAR
• Focus on the few critical issues. • Do it as soon as possible after the action in question. • Include the whole group. • Do it in a structured way each time. • Put the lessons to use as soon as possible.	• What did we set out to do? • What actually happened? • What did or can we learn from this? • What do we do now? • Who else should we tell?

It is useful to include the whole team in the AAR process. It might take people away from their jobs for an hour or two and use up time, but it will usually be worth it. By including the whole group, you are more likely to get a full perspective. It will also send an implicit signal that the contribution of every individual is important and that everyone must thus be alert to what is not working as well as it could, and to be ready to adapt in response.

In perspective: A perpetual and multidimensional process of influence

In summing up, let's note four main points.

To begin with, one of the most important features of the military team style is the multiplicity of ways in which leaders build cohesion, trust and a sense of agency. Recall how Russell Linwood would routinely introduce visitors to a team member by talking about the ways in which that member had contributed to performance (see Chapter 7). This single action would have brought a number of benefits: helping those colleagues to feel good about themselves and about Linwood; reminding all concerned of the relevance/importance of the activity that was being singled out; and demonstrating to that colleague (and probably to others) that Linwood was in touch with what was going on.

Secondly, one of the military leadership style's great strengths is the uniformity and consistency with which it is applied, even though leaders might differ in how they apply its principles. Such consistency helps to make those at the lower levels feel comfortable that, regardless of who is in charge, their style of leadership will be broadly similar to those who went before and those who will come later.

Thirdly, the three main components of military leadership culture—ethos, professional practices and teamwork—are mutually reinforcing. A core set of principles and values guide individuals in their practice of leadership and this in turn reinforces those values for both the individual and the team.

Finally, as has been mentioned a number of times, leading can be fun as well as useful. Managers who lead well invariably enjoy their work more, a point that doesn't get the recognition it deserves. Professor John McCallum was one of the former national services officers who mentioned this. 'I can work with people and get them working together, I relish the excitement of leading so much more than I think most of my academic peers do.'

The next chapter describes the way the Australian Army develops its leaders, embedding and standardising the principles by which people lead.

A final illustration

We close with a popular image from a Shakespearean play filled with examples of, and allusions to, leadership. Many people will be familiar with two well-known rallying speeches in *Henry V*: 'Once more unto the breach, dear friends . . .', which the king makes at a critical point during the Battle of Harfleur, and 'We few, we happy few, we band of brothers' before the Battle of Agincourt.

But, there's an alternative image elsewhere in the play of the king-as-leader that, while less well known, is much more pertinent to the leadership processes discussed in the last few chapters.

It is the night before Agincourt. The English force is significantly outnumbered and, after many tough weeks in the field, morale is somewhat shaky. Henry deals with this not with stirring words, but by quietly moving among his men and conversing with them—man to man—as they huddle around their campfires. It is perhaps telling that the Bard uses the name 'Harry' to refer to the king in these scenes: more a prototypical Englishman than an all-powerful monarch.

> With cheerful semblance and sweet majesty;
> That every wretch, pining and pale before,
> Beholding him, plucks comfort from his looks:
> A largess universal, like the sun,
> His liberal eye does give to every one,
> Thawing cold fear, that mean and gentle all
> Behold (as may unworthiness define)
> A little touch of Harry in the night.

By his actions and by his mere presence—much more so than by his words—Henry demonstrates his unity with his common soldiers, his concern for their welfare and his intention to serve them faithfully: in short, his mission-oriented, team-oriented, servant leadership ethic.

9

BUILDING AN ORGANISATION BY BUILDING ITS PEOPLE

It takes a village to raise a child.

African proverb

The more I practise, the luckier I get.

Gary Player, South African golfing champion

Worth its weight in black gold

A few years ago I was contracted to do some organisational survey work for one of the world's most successful companies, Schlumberger Oilfield Exploration.

Even though I'd had no previous experience with my new client, I felt on curiously familiar ground almost as soon as I began. I could not understand why at first, but then the penny dropped. Schlumberger's approach to career and leadership development was very similar to that of the Army's.

Many of the company's career executives were former engineers who had been recruited from universities all over the world at the start of their careers. They then attended a lengthy company finishing school in order to learn 'the Schlumberger way' before going into the field in remote and often politically unstable environments to head up small teams of skilled blue-collar technicians, supported in each case by an experienced foreman. After several years of this, and after various company leadership courses in one of its central locations, most had been promoted to general management positions, often in non-engineering fields such as marketing and personnel. In such roles, they acted in the leader-as-catalyst mode, eliciting the best from their specialised staff and aligning those specialist functions with the company's broader intent and strategic perspective.

Just as importantly, Schlumberger regarded the leadership function, as did the Army, as integral to business success. The company saw leadership as 'everybody's business' and the process of leadership development was continuous, structured around both everyday opportunities and formal programs.

Schlumberger's success continues, with revenues in the 2015/16 financial year of more than US$35 billion.

Army leadership development

Effective leadership—the process of engaging the concerted efforts of willing followers—depends on both skill and will.

The primary focus in this chapter is the second element. Willingness—indeed, desire and urge—to lead owes at least as much to a person's character and values, sense of responsibility, self-confidence, and personal and professional identity as it does to their competence. The military's focus on these less tangible elements of leadership effectiveness is one of the main differentiators between it and the vast majority of civilian organisations.

Moreover, aside from its role in decision-making and adaptability, the 'skill element' is an important foundation for motivation and willpower. Skills are the indispensable foundation for decision-making and adaptability and are part of the basis by which would-be leaders demonstrate their potential for representing and being accepted by a group. And a person's self-perceived skill level is an important contributor to his/her confidence when stepping forward and leading other practitioners within that craft.

We begin by looking at the core strategy of sowing early and planting deeply and widely in order to shape identity, character and values, and learning orientation. Then we look at some subtle but essential features that make experiential learning effective.

Sow early and plant deeply and widely

Good leadership development is like sensible agriculture. To grow a crop that will bear healthy fruit for years to come, take advantage of the fertile and malleable soil of youth, then sow early and plant deeply and widely in a range of paddocks.

Keep one important point in mind as we move through the discussion that follows. The process of developing individual *leaders* simultaneously develops *leadership* as an organisational attribute. The processes by which people develop important skills and aspects of character also help them to learn to work together and see the world from a variety of perspectives.

Junior officer career development begins with several years of intensive learning experiences that give young professionals the appropriate know-how for their role and embeds the leadership ethos discussed in Chapter 4.

For most people this commences during the university program at the tri-service Australian Defence Force Academy (ADFA). Formal and informal military-specific leadership-learning activities are conducted during university breaks. For example, Army cadets learn the basic skills of soldiering, including weapons handling and field craft. Such activities, together with the trappings of Academy life, also serve as a continual reminder of what they should aspire to. (Their Navy and Air Force peers undergo equivalent development.)

For Army cadets, tertiary studies are followed by another year of intensive professional military training at the Royal Military College, Duntroon. This is topped off by several weeks of intensive training in their chosen speciality—for example, infantry, artillery, signals, logistics, etc.—before assignment to a unit of their professional speciality where they start putting it all into practice. (Again, the Navy and the Air Force have equivalent programs.)

Take the early career development experiences of the average cadet. He begins his career at the Defence Force Academy, choosing from a range of disciplines, including economics, history, science, mathematics and engineering. (Given that 83 per cent of Australia's Army officers are men, it will typically be 'he'.) During the academic year, he will focus on his university studies with military training activities undertaken during semester breaks. After graduation he will attend a year-long program at Duntroon in which he will expand his understanding of the basics of leadership and officership. He will study leadership theory, with particular focus on historical and contemporary case studies. An important part of this will be to become familiar with the Army's 'two-up two-down' approach to thinking about and studying leadership. Thus he will be schooled in the activities and perspectives of three levels of organisation: the roles that he will fill in the two or three years after graduation (typically commanding a platoon), the responsibilities and perspectives one and two levels higher (that is, company and battalion command), and those one and two levels lower (platoon sergeant and section commander). All this helps him to appreciate how his decisions will relate to and affect others in organisational change, and how the decisions of others will affect him.

On graduation from Duntroon as, say, an infantryman, he will attend a shorter and intensive course at the Infantry Centre in NSW, further broadening and deepening his understanding of his chosen craft. He will then be assigned to an infantry battalion, where his company commander will be alert for any experience, no matter how minor, that will help his young charge to polish and practise his skills and expand his perspectives.

In those early career years he will be particularly encouraged to take every opportunity to learn about leadership. His supervisors will make it clear to their young officers that 'honest failure' is acceptable, provided that they learn from the experience. This will encourage him to face challenges that he might otherwise dodge for fear of looking foolish or inadequate, and for which he will be mentored by his various company commanders and platoon sergeants. His skill and confidence will steadily and constructively expand.

Over the next few years he will attend many training and educational programs to expand various professional skill sets. As he becomes more senior, such courses will become less frequent but generally longer. He will perhaps attend an overseas program, such as at the US Army Infantry School at Fort Benning. Midway through his second decade of service, he will attend a one-year military staff college course, either in Australia or, if he is lucky, overseas.

Steadily but imperceptibly, his perspective of leadership will shift from a 'me-as-rule-follower' (appropriate to a young leader who is a cog in a much larger machine) into 'me-as-rule-maker' (appropriate to a unit leader who plays an important role within that machine). If he advances into the high levels of his profession, this will shift to the even broader perspective of 'me-as-system-builder.'

An important part of this total learning experience will be its effect on the less tangible aspects of professional effectiveness, in terms of identity, character, values and learning orientation.

Intangible targets of professional development

Military career and leadership development aims not only at the development of competencies but also at identity, character and values, and learning orientation.

Identity

Identity (or self-image or self-concept) refers to how you define yourself to yourself and to the world; the way that you conceive of your distinctive capabilities; and what you value, deep down. In short: who you think you are.

Most people don't think about their identity and how it influences their behaviour very much, or even at all. No matter: whether it is implicit or explicit, the way in which you define yourself shapes what you do, the choices you make and the way you see the world, and your persistence in the face of real or imagined challenges.

We instinctively tend to behave in ways that are consistent with our sense of who we are and what we stand for. We seek opportunities to do things that confirm and strengthen our sense of self, and we are often uncomfortable when we are required to 'act out of character'. By continually reminding us of our duties and obligations as a 'leader', a strong sense of identity keeps us focused in situations where physical fatigue or mental distraction would normally impede appropriate performance.

And if you perceive yourself in these terms, you will feel a deep sense of satisfaction when you are 'in role', which further reinforces appropriate behaviour.

Leadership-identity development in the Army often begins even before successful candidates are officially enlisted. Officer candidates attend a selection process that culminates in a day-long set of group and individual assessment activities. One of its memorable aspects is the outdoor problem-solving exercise. In small groups, candidates are set a task that cannot be properly solved—for example, to move a heavy drum over barriers using little more than a few wooden poles. As the teams go about their task, those who are assessing them look for evidence of collaboration, coolness, determination, insight and other indicators of leadership potential. (Recklessness is not well regarded: anyone who jumps up with the cry of 'Follow me!' is often marked down.) For successful candidates, it will be one of the earliest affirmations of their growing sense of themselves as someone with leadership potential.

Once they begin their service, skill acquisition occurs in parallel with the development of such 'softer' attributes. The two parallel elements often reinforce each other. The more young cadets and officers learn about military life and the skills involved, the more they are drawn to seeing themselves as particular kinds of people; and this in turn motivates them to learn the deeper intricacies of their broader profession, further embedding the sense of identity and thirst for learning that are at the core of the leadership ethos discussed in Chapter 4.

Junior leadership presents one of the most formidable 'stepping-up' career stages. The process of leading tends to be unfamiliar to most people, and requires an extrovert projection of self, which sometimes poses at least a few problems for those who are not extroverts, as we saw in Chapter 7. A strong personal sense of 'me as a leader' helps you to overcome anxieties and to engage with the team.

Moreover, seeing the world through a 'leader's' eyes helps you to be more tuned into what is going on in terms of leadership implications. Those whose sense of identity includes a leadership element will be more inclined to look beyond immediate issues and think about broader opportunities and problems. They also tend to be more attuned to the responsibilities associated with leadership, in terms of both leading from the front and supporting their colleagues elsewhere in the network.

Character and values

Skills may be superseded by other skills, but character and values will not. And the ideal life stage in which to embed attributes such as a strong sense of responsibility, integrity, confidence and resilience is when learners are still feeling their way in the world.

The development of character poses greater challenges than the development of competency. The process is much more nebulous, not least because the effects of such development are difficult to measure. As a consequence, character development is often taken for granted until there is evidence of the contrary—by which stage it can be too late.

Those who supervise young officers will usually be alert to appropriate opportunities for assessing and discussing character factors in their junior charges. Such opportunities will range from classic military history case studies through to something that happened recently in that or another unit. In this way, young officers are continually reminded of the importance of integrity and resolve, both for longer-term performance and success and also for maintaining their reputations and for fulfilling their obligations to their junior colleagues.

National serviceman Ray Williams was one of many whose civilian career benefited from such development. He recalls an example that he regards as evidence of this: as a young manager, he was asked to 'back-date and rewrite' a report on an employee in order to avoid embarrassment to the company. But he took the attitude of 'stiff shit' and stood his ground. Although 'it cost the company a bit of money in the short term' and made him 'not flavour of the month for a while', he regards it as having been 'worth it', and he credits his character development and guidance as a young officer for this aspect of his professionalism.

Learning orientation

Learning orientation refers to how individuals view new learning experiences. Do they have an 'exploratory' orientation, whereby they relish challenges as opportunities to learn and be stretched, even if they stumble a little in doing so? Or do they have a risk-averse or 'protective' orientation, whereby they see challenges as threats to their sense of competence? Research shows that those who have an exploratory perspective tend to grow and perform better in the long run, with their tendency to seek new challenges resulting in progressive development of their skills, perspectives and confidence. In contrast, those who regard challenges as opportunities to 'look good', or as threats to their sense of self, will be less willing to step forward to meet future challenges.

Many people don't like to operate out of their comfort zones, especially in challenging roles like leadership. Those best equipped to do so regard new challenges as opportunities to learn and grow rather than to 'look good' or confirm their existing identity.

Some people are naturally exploratory and others are naturally protective, but most of us begin with the potential to be encouraged—directly and indirectly—in either direction.

It is perhaps no surprise that many of the most successful former national servicemen returned to their civilian careers with a strong exploratory orientation. Peter Whitelaw went on to a successful career in engineering, general management and management consultancy. He sees his habit of seeking opportunities for self-improvement and experience as an important factor in his subsequent career success. Whitelaw regards his military experience as being so 'crucial' in this respect. Since he knew he wasn't in it for the long term, it didn't really matter to him if he made mistakes as a junior officer, so 'I gave it a go and, in the process, gained the self-discipline and tenacity that were probably latent but needed to be brought out'.

Much depends on the trust and support given by your immediate superior. If the boss is focused on things being done 'by the book', without allowing you room to stretch yourself and see what you can do, you are likely to develop a protective orientation. But while this might serve you well in the short term—that is, with that boss—it's likely to be a less successful strategy in the long run. Wise bosses nurture enterprise and curiosity.

Over the decades, the military has devised a reliable formula for career development and it sticks to this approach. For example, it occasionally thinks about accelerating promotion for exceptional officers, but it always resists such a policy on a number of grounds, including the downsides of pushing people too fast too early and of depriving officers of the crucial (not to mention deeply satisfying) experiences associated with command at the successive levels of the profession.

Professor John McCallum, whom we met in previous chapters, was one of many former national service officers who came to value the leadership skills—'basic though they were'—he had picked up in his time in uniform. They gave him a way of thinking and a level of confidence that he thinks is lacking in most of his contemporaries. He found that he could readily 'think team', get people working together, and judge 'who and when to let loose'. In contrast, most of his peers tended to 'move chips around the board without any real purpose and outcome'. McCallum views this as 'not surprising', since most of those peers were 'products of working for bosses just like them: people whose first decade or so of professional life was totally focused on technical matters, and who came to leadership roles comparatively late and thus without any significant preparation'. As a consequence, they 'tried to do it all by themselves when they could rarely bring it off'. McCallum's early career experience gave him a distinct perspective on his role as well as the ability to work with people and, as a result, 'I can keep calm and focused and get people working together.'

The vital ingredients

Useful learning is most likely to happen when learning experiences are *challenging*, allow the learner appropriate *autonomy*, and are supported by managers and supervisors who give relevant *feedback and support*. And as shown in the brief discussion below, each of these elements has to be 'just right': too much or too little either nullifies or significantly reduces the value of the experience involved.

Challenge

The effectiveness of a work assignment as a learning experience depends very much on the degree of challenge involved. Too little and young leaders will learn little, because they are not taken out of their comfort zones. Too much and they are likely to be overwhelmed.

The process never really stops. Comparatively short and highly structured early career experiences and courses give way to longer and greater mid- and late-career challenges, often overseas or on assignment to a civilian organisation. Whatever their level, ambitious leaders should continuously push their own learning boundaries and play their part in nurturing others.

Former national serviceman Neville Gale became a successful businessman and executive, but he regards his first leadership challenge as a platoon commander as one of his most important. He was with his platoon on patrol in heavy rain and swampy terrain. Although there were some 'rumblings' from some of the soldiers that the platoon had become lost, Gale was fairly confident that it had not. Prior to returning to the base camp, he called in the section commanders and asked each for the platoon's current map reference. 'All three gave slightly different locations and all three were wrong,' he says. 'After showing them our correct position and our route home, I could hear the audible disbelief—and relief!—when, in fading light, we came out of the jungle precisely at our base.' He still laughs about it with those former soldiers and their families when they meet regularly at platoon reunions. The important lesson that he learned that day was 'to stick to my guns when I knew that I was right'. And Gale learned another and equally important lesson that night: 'The best results are often achieved by sometimes taking risks. Standing still waiting for something to happen is never an option.'

Autonomy

It is also important to achieve the outcome alone and largely unaided. You will learn the most when task achievement is essentially down to you rather than to others. At the same time, you need the right balance of autonomy. Leaving somebody on their own for too long can be so stressful that they risk developing an aversion for such situations in the future.

Former national serviceman and later mining executive Don Ramsay recalls the 'real challenge' of being acting company commander as a 21-year-old. He now realises 'how clueless I was at the time, and how little I understood about what a company commander was supposed to do'. But he worked through it and now regards it as one of the most important experiences in his development as a leader. The key factor was that he had just the right amount of autonomy: he did not have to act completely independently because he had 'a little help from friends', in the form of advice and counselling from his battalion commander above and his company sergeant major below. All young leaders, he says, should be fortunate enough to be granted the same support.

After his military service, Peter Graham was another who always worked on the principle that a young leader needs to have the confidence to fail. He cites an example of when he was head of human resources for Pacific Power. He had appointed a promising junior colleague to act in a position for four weeks. Halfway through that month 'she came into my office, white with anxiety, to tell me that she had made an error on a compo claim which was going to cost the company \$60,000'. Graham was quick to reassure her. 'The company has just spent \$60,000 on your development. It's OK to fail but you have to learn from it.'

Feedback and support

Feedback and support are important factors in learning. If you have the good fortune to receive feedback and support from a trusted source, make the most of it. As we have seen in many of the stories in preceding chapters, a wiser head can assist us in assessing what worked and what didn't, what we need to keep doing, and what we need to change or improve.

Ernie Bryon remembers—with rueful embarrassment—his autocratic approach when he began working with soldiers. If things didn't get done to his satisfaction, he would dress them down and sometimes charge them, even though he knew instinctively that it 'wasn't the best way to do things'. His battery commander (BC), Major Mike Crawford, gradually guided him into a different approach. 'The BC had a very distinctive approach to giving feedback,' Bryon recalls. 'He would observe you doing something, but then often talk to you about it after a day or two, when you would have cooled down.' In such follow-up sessions, Crawford would probe him with questions such as: 'Was that the best way to deal with it? How else could you have handled that?' Knowing that the BC was likely to do this encouraged Bryan to develop what turned out to be a lifelong habit of continual reflection and follow-up. The payoff after his return to BHP was almost immediate. 'I had a constructive approach to interpersonal dealings that coincided with the way the company began moving in the 1970s and '80s, and I soon found that I was getting the promotions.'

Feedback doesn't have to come from those above you. Peter Morgan is a former national serviceman and teacher who later became a conservation activist. Early in his experience as a young officer, he had 'a very candid conversation with my sergeant one day'. Morgan recalls how the sergeant 'took me around the back and told me that if I continued to be the directive autocrat that I was shaping up to be, I would have a rebellion on my hands'. It was tough feedback for a young man to take on, but it had a huge benefit. 'It caused me to really think about what I was there for and how I should approach my task of leadership.' Every young leader, he says, should be so lucky.

However, just as with too much challenge, too much feedback can be overwhelming, especially if most of it involves criticism. A good supervisor or mentor will follow the Toastmasters' rule: begin by noting something the learner did well and should continue to do, then follow that up with no more than three comments on what he or she should improve ('points for improvement'), then close with a final encouraging remark.

Onwards

The military regards leader development and career development as synonymous. Leadership capability expands as the career expands, with individuals moving more or less seamlessly from the narrow focus of the junior role into the broader and deeper perspectives of those at higher levels.

The Army is particularly strong in its approach to early and mid-career development, where a set of programs provide a solid foundation that many other organisations lack. Any big organisation that is concerned about performance and agility should consider a similar approach.

This is confirmed by the many former national servicemen who went on to careers in private enterprise. Peter Graham, whose experiences have repeatedly been cited in earlier chapters, is one who recognises the continued validity of the military's programs. They are enduring, he says, 'because they work'.

Sowing early, planting deeply and widely: this is the strategy for embedding the seeds of the leadership identity in promising young professionals. Then nurture the shoots that spring up with a mixture of guided experience and structured programs. And then reap the rewards in terms of an improved organisational culture.

10

IT'S THE BACKSWING, STUPID

How well you lead, how sharp your own personal
discipline ... will be largely influenced by how
you approached soldiering back in barracks when
training for war. Most important of all is how
you mastered 'personal example', for with any
leader, no matter how professional he may appear,
all will be lost if he is not prepared to lead by
personal example.

Australian Army, Junior Leadership on the Battlefield

You may be the strongest man in the world, or have
hands that can tear a telephone book in two, but
neither ability is going to be an asset in golf unless
you can learn to utilise the relevant muscles in a
rhythmical and harmonious way.

Peter Thomson, Australian golfing legend

Applying the principles

The new CO assumed her regimental command soon after the misogynistic backlash to greater female inclusion in the military that prompted the now well-known video message in which Lieutenant General David Morrison laid down the law. As the first woman to command a regiment within her military specialisation, she was determined to do well, not just for herself but also, just as importantly, for the generation of female officers who would follow. But, however much she and her peers were supported by the chief, she knew that success would be largely up to her, so she focused on the leadership practices that had become habitual across her years of service: building relationships with her soldiers, observing and joining in team training activities, discussing professional matters with them and, in many other ways, quietly and subtly demonstrating her experience and professional competence. She vividly remembers the moment she knew she was on track. It was during an exercise, several months after she assumed command, when she was doing the rounds of the various forward positions of the regiment. As she was about to leave one outpost, the corporal in charge farewelled her with a seemingly offhand remark: 'We reckon that you're alright, boss.' It was a moment she will never forget.

The military's world is one of volatility, uncertainty, complexity and ambiguity; an often dangerous environment where people must perform at the highest possible level despite psychological and physical conditions that would challenge élite sportspeople; a world in which, as I once heard an experienced infantry officer put it, leaders and followers alike 'must perform at their best on their very worst day'. Excellence in leadership practice is not simply a competitive advantage: it is fundamental to the way the military operates and thinks about itself.

The Army practises a distinctive form of leadership at both the operational and team levels. It is organised as a networked hierarchy, in which leaders act as catalysts for the performance of others. Leadership at all levels is typically values-driven and based on the practices provided in the 3Rs model. The skills and values on which this style depend are developed through processes that begin at the earliest possible stage, with development directed as much at intangible attributes—such as identity, responsibility, character and values—as at professional and executive skills.

And while the task of leading is a perpetual challenge, it is one that inspires deep satisfaction and pride in those involved, spurring them on to reach higher and wider. It is little wonder that the institution as a whole consistently does leadership well.

A highly transferable set of practices

Chapter 5 concluded with a simple axiom. In leadership terms— as with many other areas of life—the more you know, the better you'll go. This book will help you to analyse and lift your leadership game. Like the many former and currently serving service people whose experiences have been drawn upon, you can apply its various ideas in a range of fields at both the individual and the organisational level.

At the *individual* level:

- Regard yourself as a leader—in fact, as 'a leader first'—and work on leadership as your primary professional competence, seeing the world through a leader's eyes in order to spot opportunities and challenges well before others do, and working through others to get things done.

- Use the 3Rs model as a mental 'app' for day-to-day self-monitoring, reflection, self-development and self-critiquing.
- Never stop learning about and reflecting on leadership, no matter how experienced you become.
- Use your team as a personal learning resource. If you want to know how you are performing, ask them. As Australians, it is likely they will treat your honesty and humility with corresponding respect. They will appreciate being asked and they will appreciate having a boss who wants to perform better in order to run the team more effectively.

At the *organisational* level:

- Sow the leadership seed early, deeply and widely, as part of career and leadership development programs.
- Ensure you concentrate on leadership capability at all levels, from leaders of frontline teams to budding executives.
- Give those leaders the skills and perspectives that will enable them to see themselves and act as catalysts, rather than as controllers.
- Build a sense of common identity. Begin at the team level and work up to the organisation. Make people proud to belong as well as conscious of the organisation's heritage and values. Never forget the principle of 'leadership as a team sport'.

- Morph this approach into the networked form the military finds so useful: teams of teams, grouped to suit the circumstances and capable of ready reformation as the situation changes.

But however you apply these ideas, hold to the principles of *preparation* and *consistency*. As the opening quote of this chapter asserts, good leadership is not something you can turn on at a moment's notice and with comparatively little practice. It stems from a foundation for thinking and practice, a foundation that must be built well in advance of its being needed. Its various activities must be applied consistently so they become so habitual that you can draw upon them regardless of how much stress you are under, and so your team will become accustomed to positive and reliable leadership.

Less direct forms of leadership influence

Although this book's focus is the leadership of teams, the principles apply equally to any grouping. Whether that team is a rifle section, battalion, brigade or division—or a factory floor, manufacturing department, corporation, or all their equivalents across different industries—your effectiveness in generating followership depends on the degree to which you can represent, relate to and run your team(s). The processes might vary but the principles will not.

For reasons of space, this book has not discussed two other modes of leadership influence—*leading from the shadows* and *leading from the top*. 'Leading from the shadows' is my term for a process known as social and political acumen. It comprises the skills needed to make sense of, and influence, people in situations involving multiple stakeholders with diverse and sometimes competing interests. A recent study shows that such skills depend on using personal and interpersonal skills to interact constructively with others, building relationships and networks, reading people and situations, and thinking and acting strategically. Interested readers may find some value in my recent paper in the *Australian Defence Force Journal*, 'Social and political acumen: A vital but neglected professional skill set'.

Leading from the top—strategic leadership—is essentially about making decisions and establishing plans and capabilities today with the clear intention of them becoming the instruments of performance tomorrow. Effective strategic leadership also depends on the ability to discern and interpret broad longer-term issues and trends, particularly in terms of their implications for intellectual and social capital, as well as for more tangible organisational assets in the form of structural capital. Interested readers may find some value in my recent book on the topic, *The Chiefs* (2013), which is available for download on the Defence website.

'It's the backswing, stupid'

We conclude with a metaphor that illustrates many of the points made in this chapter.

A leadership culture has the same kind of effect on organisational performance as a backswing has in golf. Without a sound golf swing, it is difficult to score consistently well, and without a sound leadership culture, it is difficult for leaders to lead consistently well.

To put it simply: 'It's the backswing, stupid.'

I formulated this principle during a particularly tedious golf match when, as usual, I was playing poorly. To pass the time constructively, I began to think idly about the similarities between golf and leadership, particularly in the light of two things I had repeatedly noted about my fellow duffers:

- Most players have problems with their backswings. In a multitude of ways, they put themselves in positions at the tops of their backswings that then make it difficult for them to reliably complete the downswing and thus hit the ball sweetly.

- And when the inevitable bad shot results, golfers (often after a burst of profanity) invariably explain the fault in terms of their *down*swing. They will say they hadn't held their head still, had started the downswing too early, had let their hands lead their hips, blah, blah, blah. But rarely do any of these self-diagnoses have anything to do with the real cause of the problem.

The parallel with the diagnosis of organisational leadership problems is as follows:

- Just as with a backswing, the reasons for most deep-seated leadership problems in an individual or organisation usually stem from long-standing structural factors rather than from neglect or incompetence by those who happen to be in charge at the time. And even if these people are patently neglectful or incompetent, the reasons probably have much more to do with flaws in the leadership culture in which they work than with them as individuals.

- But an organisation hardly ever sees it that way. It will see the problem in terms of *delivery*—that is, the *down*swing. So it focuses on *symptoms* such as individuals failing to take charge, lack of skill, unethical practices and so on. And when an organisation focuses on fixing flaws in delivery without considering the more fundamental flaws in its structure and leadership culture—that is in the *back*swing—it simply sets itself up for continuing problems.

A long association with both golf and organisational diagnosis has taught me these twin fundamental truths:

- If you have a sound backswing, you have a better chance of consistently hitting the ball sweetly.
- If you have a supportive organisational climate, you have a better chance of consistently performing well.

This commonsense wisdom is reflected in the opening quotations in this and the previous chapter by two champions of a past era. South African golfer Gary Player reminds us that we will achieve little without a considerable amount of practice on whatever it is we want to achieve. Just as fundamentally, Australian golfing legend Peter Thomson tells us that brute strength and raw talent are far from enough, and that it is the disciplined use of both attributes in conjunction with other factors that convert promise into results.

Once I came to this realisation, I worked on my backswing. I took some lessons from a pro who shared my views on this phenomenon and, gradually, my scores improved. More importantly, I enjoyed my game more.

It was the same when I put aside my golfing interests and became a temporary community leader. My formulation of the 3Rs gave me greater insight into the dynamics of my leadership roles, and helped me deal with the multitude of challenges involved. And whenever I was tempted to look for a quick fix, I would remind myself: 'It's the backswing, stupid.'

This principle runs through all the cases that have introduced various chapters. Success in leadership is based on a strong foundation of skill, will, confidence and patience. We saw it in the manner in which Major General John Cantwell presented himself as a leader the people of disaster-struck Marysville could trust; in former Lieutenant Colonel Colin Toll's transformation of Mount Blue Cow into a standard-bearer of customer service in the Australian ski industry; in the professionalism shown by the junior soldiers in Jon Hawkins' special forces squadron in Afghanistan; in the skills and values many former national servicemen derived from their time as junior officers and applied to successful civilian careers; in the steady approach to organisational improvement used by Major Echo to improve the performance of her movement-control agency in the Middle East; in Noel Turnbull's application of the people-management practices he had learned as a junior officer in Vietnam to his business; in Lieutenant Colonel Mick King's team-oriented approach to lifting morale and performance in his logistics battalion; in the development of similar cultures of professionalism and leadership in Schlumberger and the Australian Army, two organisations that ostensibly could not be more different; and finally, at the beginning of this chapter, in a female CO's steady approach to winning the trust of her predominantly male workforce.

Leadership is a bit like exercise. You might not know how long it will take to work but you do know that getting fit requires a variety of disciplined activities. There may not be much explicit feedback on just what is working and how well it's going, especially in the early stages, but leaders who know what they are doing can be confident their efforts will pay off as long as they keep doing those right things according to the right principles.

This book sets you up for the practices and insights that will help you lift your game—individually and collectively—in the leadership arena. Take it on board. Good luck, and have fun!

Appendix 1

CONTEMPORARY ARMY STRUCTURE

This brief appendix gives some information on the structure of the contemporary Australian military, with particular reference to the Australian Army.

Mission

To fight and win the joint land battle.

Strength

The Army comprises 29,635 members serving full time in either the permanent force or as full-time reservists, and 14,500 reservists serving part time.

Structure

The Army comprises a number of corps, each of which comprises both permanent and reserve members. They include:

- Combat: Armoured, Artillery, Aviation, Electrical & Mechanical Engineers, Engineers, Infantry, Intelligence, Military Police, Ordnance, Signals, Transport.
- Support: Band, Catering, Chaplains, Dental, Educational, Legal, Medical, Nursing, Pay, Psychology, Public Relations.

The Army is structured around 'units', which are organisational elements of several hundred officers and soldiers with appropriate weapons and equipment, capable of acting independently. A unit is generally commanded by a lieutenant colonel, and will comprise a number of sub-units (companies, squadrons or batteries of up to 100 personnel), each of which will generally be commanded by a major. The sub-units in turn comprise component elements, such as platoons or troops (of around 30, commanded by lieutenants), and these in turn comprise sections (usually no more than 10, commanded by corporals). A grouping of a number of units is known as a formation—often a brigade or division.

The nomenclature associated with 'unit' will vary according to the particular corps. For example, an infantry unit is generally a 'battalion', with the units in many other corps being called 'regiments'.

Ranks

Table A1.1: Officers (commissioned)

Army	Navy equivalent	Air Force equivalent
Officer cadet	Midshipman	Officer cadet
2nd lieutenant	Acting sub lieutenant	Pilot officer
Lieutenant	Sub lieutenant	Flying officer
Captain	Lieutenant	Flight lieutenant
Major	Lieutenant commander	Squadron leader
Lieutenant colonel	Commander	Wing commander
Colonel	Captain	Group captain
Brigadier	Commodore	Air commodore
Major general	Rear admiral	Air vice marshal
Lieutenant general	Vice admiral	Air marshal
General	Admiral	Air chief marshal

Table A1.2: Other ranks (soldiers, sailors, airmen/airwomen)

Army	Navy equivalent	Air Force equivalent
Private*	Seaman	Aircraftsman
Lance corporal	Able seaman	Leading aircraftsman
Corporal	Leading seaman	Corporal
Sergeant	Petty officer	Sergeant
Staff sergeant	—	—
Warrant officer class II	Chief petty officer	Flight sergeant
Warrant officer class I	Warrant officer	Warrant officer
Regimental sergeant major of the Army	Warrant officer of the Navy	Warrant officer of the Air Force

* Gunner, trooper, craftsman, signalman, patrolman, sapper or musician, depending on the corps or regiment.

Appendix 2

MAKING THE LEADER-AS-CATALYST APPROACH WORK

Making decisions and putting them into effect

There are many skills and techniques associated with the style of team leadership described in this book. In the interests of brevity, we will concentrate on the three that many former officers regarded as essential to their subsequent career activities, and thus might be of value to other civilians. These are:

- reaching decisions with the aid of the military appreciation process;
- tasking the team by applying the principles of mission command; and
- communicating via the protocol known as SMEAC.

The military appreciation process

The military appreciation process is a systematic and disciplined approach to problem-solving and decision-making in which a situation is analysed in order to devise a considered plan.

Using the process enables you to systematically:

- scope the situation to understand the nature of the problem as clearly as possible;
- define the problem in ways that specify the outcomes you want when you want them;
- establish the aim, including any assumptions that have been made;
- identify the courses open to you, and their respective advantages and disadvantages;
- select the preferred course after weighing up the pros and cons of each; and
- outline the plan, the final step, to give a sense of how the logic hangs together.

The military appreciation process balances decisiveness with deliberation. Indeed, one of the early factors to be considered is the time available for the planning process itself. A dictum in military thinking is to allow adequate time for deciding just *what* you want to achieve before you rush into *how*. It is all too easy to settle instinctively on a particular goal because of familiarity, custom, habit or panic, and other impediments to systematic thought. The rule of thumb: if you have 30 minutes to come up with a plan, spend the first ten deciding on your goal. Don't rush into the first apparently obvious option. It is a process that is drummed into every young officer.

Enacting operations by practising 'mission command'

One of the main techniques used by military organisations to make networked hierarchy happen is the distinctive collaborative leadership process of mission command.

Mission command is a process by which a leader tasks subordinate leaders by providing them with the information, resources and freedom of action needed to tackle specific objectives within an overall plan. The leader clearly enunciates the results required, including any constraints or limitations, and those subordinate leaders are then left to get on with their parts of the operation, keeping the senior or central leader informed on progress and developments, thus freeing up that senior leader to think about, monitor and manage the broader picture.

A practical guide to what's involved was ably provided by Brigadier Roger Noble, who describes mission command as 'a philosophy of command and a system for conducting operations'. Mission command, he says, is essential for focusing effective action at the lowest possible level. 'The larger unit is then able to operate as a set of small, cohesive and highly trained groups, in which the willpower, character and ability of those in each component group determines the overall potential of the total team.' This results in 'a network of intent that binds all activities, which is the logical and best response to the challenge of complexity and chaos'.

The process is important for leaders who want to act as catalysts rather than as controllers. But for this to be effective, says

Noble, it must be built on clear intent, accountability and trust. 'The central moral component is that last component—trust.'

Moreover, trust has to work both ways: the central or nodal leader must be trusted by subordinate leaders, and that central leader in turn must trust the subordinate counterparts.

Seeing oneself as a catalyst who gets things done through others is not as easy as it sounds. As we saw in Chapter 4, ego can get in the way, as do anxiety and timidity at the other end of the scale. Again, the crucial element is the personal and professional identity of the individual leader, and their understanding of the catalyst versus controller distinction.

Communicating the plan

The third major skill that many took away from national service officership into business is the Army's method of communicating a plan or broad intent. The Army protocol for this is known by its acronym of SMEAC—standing for Situation, Mission, Execution, Administration and Logistics, and Command and Communications. It is both a sequence and an essential-content checklist.

The leader begins by putting the team in the bigger picture through a description of the *Situation*. This helps team members to see 'Why' before they are told 'What', 'How' and 'When'. An understanding of both the 'Why' and the overall context invariably enhances people's understanding of their designated contribution to the task.

The *Mission* is the leader's statement of the objective or task. 'This is what we are going to achieve.' The convention is to state this in active and positive terms, for example: 'The battalion will take Hill 360', or 'The squadron will provide immediate support to the people of bushfire-affected X-ville'.

Execution describes how the team will achieve its purpose. It begins with the General Outline, covering the activities of the team as a whole, then delves into the particular tasks for each of the team's subordinate elements.

Administration & Logistics details the support mechanisms that will be needed: supplies, transport, rations and any other element that is germane to the task at hand.

Command & Communications deals with how the team will communicate, including relevant radio networks, passwords and the like, and also any emergency command arrangements that would be needed if the team leader becomes a casualty.

Junior officers learn the protocol as part of their field command skills, and subsequently find that it is also widely applicable in other professional activities. The protocol ensures that a leader consistently:

- presents in a logical sequence;
- doesn't leave anything out; and
- helps those being briefed to anticipate what is coming next, thereby enhancing their ability to take the relevant points on board.

One of the great advantages of the various elements is that it puts people 'in the picture' so they can grasp the *why* as well as the *what*. There are significant advantages in doing so, especially when you anticipate that the plan will have to be modified once it is enacted.

All military leaders quickly learn the sad truth of the axiom that 'a plan rarely survives its first step'. And they learn that the best ways to adapt are often those located close to the action (which is where mission command comes in).

Glossary

agency The capacity of an individual or group to make choices, and to act on such choices.

authoritarian leadership A situation in which one person dictates plans, policies and procedures, decides what goals are to be achieved, and directs and controls activities, all without any meaningful participation by the subordinates. The group is expected to complete the tasks under close supervision, providing little or no input.

authoritative leadership A situation in which group influence is exercised by those who earn trust by who they are and by what they can do—that is, on the basis of their expertise rather than position power.

commanding officer (CO) the officer appointed to command a military unit. Commanding officers are authorised to exercise lawful authority and direction over those in their units, and, within the bounds of military law, are usually given wide latitude to run their units as they see fit. In this respect, commanding officers have significant responsibilities (for example, the use of force, finances, equipment, the Geneva Conventions), duties (to higher authority, mission effectiveness, duty of care to personnel), and powers (for example, discipline and punishment of personnel within certain limits of military law).

followership The ability and willingness to follow a leader.

identity A person's distinctive sense, idea or mental image of who they are and what they stand for.

inclusion The extent to which opportunities for employment and advancement in a workplace are equivalent for all demographic groups.

leader A person who is able to initiate and sustain leadership.

leader-as-catalyst A leader who, rather than directing activities in detail, facilitates the performance of others, acting as a node or centre of networks within organisational relationships; as a focal agent who helps others to make sense of what is going on and then respond accordingly, all the while being alert to the need to take closer control in crises or emergencies.

leadership The process of engaging others in concerted efforts to pursue a goal in conditions of complexity and uncertainty, or in anticipation of such conditions.

leadership ethos A way of thinking about yourself, your role and duties, and your sense of overall identity with your profession.

management An analytical, systematic and methodical process for influencing group behaviour in situations in which there is often a 'best' method.

military appreciation process A systematic and disciplined approach to problem-solving and decision-making in which a situation is analysed in order to devise a considered plan.

mission command A process by which a more senior leader tasks a subordinate leader by providing them with the information, resources and freedom of action he/she needs to tackle specific objectives within an overall plan.

morale An attitude of confidence in the mind of individuals when they identify themselves with the group, and accept and work hard to achieve group goals.

networked hierarchy A form of organisation that avoids the narrowness of stove-piping, while benefiting from a hierarchical structure's inherent simplicity and responsiveness. The focus for action and decision-making varies according to the situation. Typically comprises teams of teams, with the smaller teams operating as the building blocks of the larger configuration, with direction of the overall system shared between the various team leaders.

non-commissioned officer (NCO) An enlisted member of the armed forces holding a position of some degree of authority who has (usually) attained it by advancement from within the non-commissioned ranks.

officer A member of an armed force or uniformed service who holds a position of authority. In its broadest sense, the term includes non-commissioned officers and warrant officers but when it is used without further detail it almost always refers to commissioned officers—that is, those more senior members of a military force who derive their authority from a commission from the head of state.

servant leadership A concept of leadership based on the premise that leaders who are best able to motivate followers are those who focus least on satisfying their own personal needs and more on prioritising support for others.

SMEAC A communication protocol based on systematically covering Situation, Mission, Execution, Administration and Logistics, and Command and Communications. It is both a sequence and an essential-content checklist.

Three Block War A military conflict zone in which a single unit must be prepared to engage simultaneously in armed conflict in a first block, provide support and mentoring for indigenous forces in a second, and help with community rebuilding in a third—all the while being able to switch seamlessly between each set of activities as well as operate within each block in ways that support the other two.

trust Reliance on the integrity, strength, ability, surety, etc., of another. Trust can take the form of either *cognition trust*, based on performance-relevant cognitions such as competence, responsibility, reliability and dependability, or *affective trust*, relating to the emotional bonds between individuals and grounded upon expressions of genuine care and concern for the welfare of the other party.

values Principles or standards of behaviour that are implicitly accepted as guides to individual or collective behaviour.

Acknowledgements

Chief among those to whom I owe a significant debt is my wife and long-term business partner and muse, Judy Frazer-Jans. Not only has she always been (often inadvertently) a leadership role model but her insights into organisational behaviour and military sociology were instrumental in her going much more deeply than simple proofreading as she reviewed my progressive drafts.

Thank you to Jamie Cullens, former head of the Centre for Defence Leadership & Ethics at the Australian Defence College, who offered me Reserve duty that enabled me to get involved in contemporary leadership programs and investigate the contemporary leadership literature, thus keeping up to date with its rapid expansion.

I am also grateful to the many contributors and those who provided forms of assistance. I trust that I have both faithfully reflected their views and have drawn valid insights from them. They are (excusing ranks and titles) Paul Asbury, Jason Agius, Gordon Alexander, Gary Allan, Chris Appleton, Stu Baldwinson, Drew Bradford, Chris Brown, Ernie Bryon, Deb Butterworth, Generoso Calonge, Colin Chapman, Jim Clement, Chris Clifton, Bram Connolly, Geoff Cooper, Terry Earle, Stuart Ellis, Tim Fischer, James Floyd, Gabrielle Follett, Paul Franklin, Todd Fresi, Shane Gabriel, Neville Gale, Michael Geier, David Gillett, Patrick Gowans, Adam Gower, Warwick Graco, Peter Graham, Jon Hawkins, Duncan Hayward, Peter Hewitt, Graham Hiley, Brian ('Hori') Howard, Peter Howe, Bob Hunter, Wayne Jackson, John James, Mike Jeffery, Samantha Johnston, Natalee Johnston, Mike Keating, Angus Kennard, Jeff Kennett, Peter Kerntke, Amanda King, Mick King, Greg Laxton, Russell Linwood, John Longhurst, Nicole Longley, John McCallum, Steve McDonald, Peter McDougall, Richard Mihaich, Kate Miller, Paul Moggach, Jim Molan, Peter Morgan, Philip Morrissey, Des Mueller, Miles Newman, Roger Noble, Meegan Olding, David Pierce, Faye Plummer, Christian Porter, Don Ramsay, Geoff Ray, Gary Reidy, Mal Rerden, Clare Rhoden, Peter Robinson, Simon Roeder, Linda Rudd, Mick Ryan, Bruce Scott, Mark Scott, Rob Senior, Bob Slater, David Sloan, Alastair Sparkes, Greg Stone, Robin Stonecash, Rob Suggett, Warren Thatcher, Greg Todd, Colin Toll, Catherine Wallis, Anthony Wennerbom, Sally Westbury, Gordon Wheaton, Dick Whitaker, Peter Whitelaw, Ray Williams and Millie Yeo.

Finally, I am grateful to Allen & Unwin for publishing my work, and for the patient and constructive editorial work by Elizabeth Weiss and Rebecca Allen.

Notes

Page viii: 'A culture of adaptability is vital to survival in the armed services...'

> Michael Useem, Four lessons in adaptive leadership, *Harvard Business Review*, November 2010, p. 89.

Chapter 1

Page 1: 'I cannot understand you Australians...'

> Quoted in George Odgers, *100 Years of Australians at War*, Lansdowne Publishing, Sydney, 1999, p. 122.

Page 1: 'A key finding of the 1995 Karpin Report...'

> Josh Healy & Andrew Bevitt, Do Australian business leaders have what it takes?, *Exchange*, 2016, 2, Centre for Workplace Leadership, Melbourne University. Available from: http://fbe.unimelb.edu.au/exchange/edition2/do-australia-business-leaders-have-what-it-takes.

Page 2: 'Thus in 1918 the Australian Corps . . .'

For a summary account of Australian military accomplish-ments, see George Odgers, *100 Years of Australians at War*, op. cit.

Page 2: '. . . those ragged bloody heroes . . .'

Peter Brune, *Those Ragged Bloody Heroes: From the Kokoda Trail to Gona Beach 1942*, Allen & Unwin, Sydney, 2005.

Page 3: '. . . a way of both practising and thinking about leadership—a leadership *culture*—that is not only distinctively Australian . . .'

See, for example, *Australian Cultural Imprints at Work: 2010 and Beyond*, Innovation & Business Skills Australia, East Melbourne, 2011; Geoff Aigner & Liz Skelton, *The Australian Leadership Paradox: What it takes to lead in the Lucky Country*, Allen & Unwin, Sydney, 2013; and Edwin Trevor-Roberts, Neal M. Ashkanasy & Jeffrey C. Kennedy, The egalitarian leader: A comparison of leadership in Australia and New Zealand, *Asia Pacific Journal of Management*, 2003, 20(4), pp. 517–40. Chapter 2 cites additional evidence in support of this proposition.

Page 3: '. . . ticks all the boxes that define contemporary best practice'

The analysis in the chapters to come show that Australian military leaders (as described in the form of the 3Rs model in later chapters) typically practise the behaviours enunciated in the 'transformational leadership' model. Research on transfor-mational leadership shows it to be consistently associated with strong performance and high morale, and often with perfor-mance beyond expectations. Transformational leadership contrasts with transactional leadership, which is a style aimed at maintaining steady-state routine performance. Transactional leaders gain compliance via both rewards and punishments, whereas transformational leaders motivate through inspiration and other intrinsic factors. Seminal works on the topic include: Bernard M. Bass, *Transformational Leadership: Individual, military and educational impact*, Lawrence Erlbaum Associates, Mahwah, NJ, 1998; Bernard M. Bass, Bruce J. Avolio, Dong I. Jung & Yair Berson, Predicting unit performance by assessing transformational and transactional leadership, *Journal of Applied Psychology*, 2003, 88(2), pp. 207–18; and Bruce J. Avolio, Fred O. Walumbwa & Todd J. Weber, Leadership: Current theories, research, and future directions, *Annual Review of Psychology*, 2009, 60, pp. 421–49. The various dimensions of transformational leadership are closely related to other leadership models, such as authentic leadership and ethical leadership, and the field begs for the systematic integration that is provided by the 3Rs model. For a recent review, see Jeremy D. Meuser, William L. Gardner, Jessica E. Dinh, Jinyu E. Hu, Robert C. Liden & Robert G. Lord, A network analysis of leadership theory: The infancy of integration, *Journal of Management*, 2016, 42(5), pp. 1374–403.

Page 5: 'A recent major study by Melbourne University's Centre for Workplace Leadership . . .'

Peter Gahan, Mladen Adamovic, Andrew Bevitt, Bill Harley, Josh Healy, Jesse E. Olsen & Max Theilacker, *Leadership at Work: Do Australian leaders have what it takes?*, Centre for Workplace Leadership, University of Melbourne, Melbourne, 2016. Available at: www.workplaceleadership.com.au/app/uploads/2017/04/SAL-Report.pdf. This was the largest ever survey of leadership in Australia, using five matched survey instruments to survey almost 8,000 individuals across 2,703 organisations and 2,561 workplaces. Respondents included leaders at all levels, from CEOs downwards.

Page 5: 'While those who participate in such programs rate their performance relatively highly, the Melbourne University study found that . . .'

> Josh Healy & Andrew Bevitt, Do Australian business leaders have what it takes?, op. cit. The measures of employee performance outcomes were self-efficacy (the feeling of agency, that 'I can do it'), workplace targets, and employee engagement.

Page 5: 'Despite the greater focus on the topic, too many regard leadership as something performed by individuals, and most development programs focus on too few people too late in their careers . . .'

> Gideon Haigh, Bad company: The cult of the CEO, *Quarterly Essay 10*, Black Inc., Melbourne, June 2003.

Page 7: '. . . when specific practices are examined closely, as they were in the 2011/12 investigations into sexual harassment . . .'

> *Review into the Treatment of Women in the Australian Defence Force, Phase 2 Report*, Australian Human Rights Commission 2012 (The Broderick Review). Available at: https://defence review.humanrights.gov.au/sites/default/files/adf-complete.pdf.

Page 8–9: '. . . as when senior people like Lieutenant General David Morrison call out unacceptable professional behaviour . . .'

> As asserted by Lieutenant General David Morrison, AO, in his video address to the Army (available at: www.youtube.com/watch?v=QaqpoeVgr8U).

Page 10: 'Happy families are all alike; every unhappy family is unhappy in its own way . . .'

> Leo Tolstoy, *Anna Karenina*.

Chapter 2

Page 13: 'Your Excellency, on behalf of a grateful Army . . .'

Army: The Newspaper for Soldiers, 15 March 2001, p. 1.

Page 13: 'Intelligent, physically superior, adaptable . . .'

Sir John Monash, *The Australian Victories in France in 1918*, Black Inc., Melbourne, 2015, pp. 291–3.

Page 14: 'Jon (Irish) Hawkins' Special Forces squadron was tasked with . . .'

Personal communication, July 2017.

Page 15: 'Even though leadership is one of the social sciences' most examined phenomena . . .'

David V. Day & John Antonakis, Leadership: Past, present, and future, in David V. Day & John Antonakis (eds), *The Nature of Leadership*, 2nd edn, Sage, Thousand Oaks, CA, 2012, p. 5.

Page 15: Definitions of 'leadership' and 'leaders'.

These are adapted from various works, including the chapter by Day and Antonakis cited above, and Richard L. Daft, *The Leadership Experience*, 7th edn, Cengage Learning, Melbourne, 2018. The definition of 'followership' is adapted from Robert E. Kelley, In praise of followers, *Harvard Business Review*, November–December 1988, pp. 142–8.

Page 16: 'values-based leadership . . .'

Michael E. Brown & Linda K. Treviño, Is values-based leadership ethical leadership?, in Stephen W. Gilliland, Dirk D. Steiner & Daniel P. Skarlicki, *Emerging Perspectives on Values in Organizations*, IAP, Greenwich, CT, 2003, pp. 151–73.

Mary Copeland, The emerging significance of values based leadership: A literature review, *International Journal of Leadership Studies*, 2014, 8(2), pp. 105–35.

David Graber & Ann Kilpatrick, Establishing values-based leadership and value systems in healthcare organizations, *Journal of Health and Human Services Administration*, 2008, 31(2), pp. 179–97.

Anne Reilly & Sara Ehlinger, Choosing a values-based leader. An experiential exercise, *Journal of Management Education*, 2007, 31(2), pp. 245–62.

Milton Rokeach, *The Nature of Human Values*, The Free Press, New York, 1973.

See also the definition of values-based leadership in the Financial Times' Lexicon, available from: http://lexicon. ft.com/Term?term=values_based-leadership; definition and values and examples available from: http://www.skills2lead. com/definition-of-values.html; Harry M. Jansen Kraemer Jr, The Only True Leadership Is Values-Based Leadership, in *Forbes* (April 26 2011), available from: https://www.forbes. com/2011/04/26/values-based-leadership.html#2d72c18a652b; Brent Gleeson, How Values-Based Leadership Transforms Organizational Cultures, in *Inc.* (March 7 2017), available from: https://www.inc.com/brent-gleeson/how-values-based-leadership-transforms-organizational-cultures.html.

Page 18: '. . . as evolutionist Professor Mark Pagel of the University of Reading puts it . . .'

Mark Pagel, *Wired for Culture: The natural history of human cooperation*, Penguin Books, London, 2012, pp. 71–2.

Page 19: '. . . leaders who were not only technically competent but could also build a sense of shared identity and unity . . .'

S. Alexander Haslam, Stephen D. Reicher & Michael J. Platow, *The New Psychology of Leadership: Identity, influence and power*, Psychology Press, Hove, East Sussex, 2011.

Page 19: 'The narrative for mainstream Australia goes back to the late eighteenth and early nineteenth centuries . . .'

> John Hirst, *Australian History in 7 Questions*, Black Inc., Melbourne, 2014: '. . . less "a penal colony" than "a colony of convicts"' (p. 27); '. . . frequently used as overseers and police, and for various professional functions . . .' (p. 31); '. . . to stop looking for eligible free people' (p. 31).

Page 20: 'All such factors created a national society that favours inclusive, supportive and egalitarian relationships . . .'

> Geoff Aigner & Liz Skelton, *The Australian Leadership Paradox: What it takes to lead in the Lucky Country*, op. cit.

Page 20: '"There is no place for difference in the Australian book of etiquette", says journalist Nick Cater . . .'

> Nick Cater, *The Lucky Culture and the Rise of an Australian Ruling Class*, HarperCollins, Sydney, 2013, p. 13. (Cater is a former editor of *The Weekend Australian*.)

Page 20: '. . . but also rarely hesitate to question directions that don't make sense . . .'

> Colin Rymer, 'Leadership in Australia—how different are we?', 2008, DBA thesis, Southern Cross University, Lismore, NSW, p. ii.

Page 21: 'This spirit would have been reinforced by the all-volunteer nature of the First Australian Imperial Force (1st AIF).'

> Jeffrey Grey, *A Military History of Australia*, Cambridge University Press, Cambridge, 1990. See p. 115.

Page 21: 'The effects of doing so are reflected in the observations of veterans and historians . . .'

> Clare Rhoden, *The Purpose of Futility: Writing World War I, Australian style*, UWA Publishing, Perth, 2015. See pp. 190 and

213; Clare Rhoden, Another perspective on Australian discipline in the Great War: The egalitarian bargain, *War in History*, 2012, 19(4), pp. 445–63.

Page 21: '. . . summed up well by the former Australian officer . . .'

G.D. Mitchell, *Backs to the Wall: A larrikin on the Western Front*, Allen & Unwin, Sydney, 2007, p. 125.

Page 22: '. . ."less ready to comply with activities perceived as extraneous". . .'

Clare Rhoden, *The Purpose of Futility: Writing World War I, Australian style*, op. cit., p. 204.

Page 22: 'You might have imagined . . .'

Gavan Daws, *Prisoners of the Japanese: POWs of World War II in the Pacific*, Scribe Publications, Carlton North, 2004, pp. 144–5. Quoted in Andrew Leigh, *Battlers and Billionaires: The story of inequality in Australia*, Redback, Schwartz Media, Melbourne, 2013, pp. 1–2.

Page 23: '. . . the Australian Cultural Imprints Studies . . .'

Australian Cultural Imprints at Work: 2010 and beyond, op. cit., 'Captain-coach leadership' and its importance for quality are introduced on p. 8 of that report, together with the contrasting leadership styles. See also Neal M. Ashkanasy, The Australian enigma, in J.S. Chhokar, F.C. Brodbeck & R.J. House (eds), *Culture and Leadership Across the World: A GLOBE report of in-depth studies of the cultures of 25 societies*, Lawrence Erlbaum Associates, Mahwah, NJ, 2007, pp. 299–333; G. Casimir & Z. Li, Combinative aspects of leadership style: A comparison of Australian and Chinese followers, *Asian Business & Management*, 2005, 4(3), pp. 271–91; N.T. Feather, Values and national identification: Australian evidence, *Australian Journal of Psychology*, 1994,

46(1), pp. 35–40; A.A. Pekerti & S. Sendjaya, Exploring servant leadership across cultures: A comparative study in Australia and Indonesia, *The International Journal of Human Resource Management*, 2010, 21(5), pp. 754–80; and Edwin Trevor-Roberts, Neal M. Ashkanasy & Jeffrey C. Kennedy, The egalitarian leader: A comparison of leadership in Australia and New Zealand, op. cit.

Page 24: 'Brigadier Shane Gabriel . . .'

A video made by Australian Defence Force media of the then Lieutenant Colonel Gabriel when he was CO of Australia's Mentoring Reconstruction Task Force in Afghanistan in 2008–09 (www.youtube.com/watch?v=SikN8p7ElBM).

Page 24: '. . . "the Three Block War" . . .'

A term attributed to US Marine Corps General Charles C. Krulak, in The strategic corporal: Leadership in the Three Block War, *Marines Magazine*, 28 January 1999, pp. 28–34.

Page 25: '. . . "taking the principles of war and applying them to peace" . . .'

Peter Kieseker, Non-government organisations, in Hugh Smith (ed.), *Peacekeeping: Challenges for the future*, Australian Defence Forces Study Centre, Australian Defence Force Academy, Canberra, 1993, pp. 57–8. See also Chris Masters, *Uncommon Soldier: Brave, compassionate and tough, the making of Australia's modern diggers*, Allen & Unwin, Sydney, 2012, pp. 314–16.

Page 25: 'Historians now regard what those soldiers did as "exceptional" . . .'

Robert Breen & Greg MacCauley, *The World Looking Over Their Shoulders: Australian Strategic Corporals on operations in Somalia and East Timor*, Land Warfare Studies Centre Papers, No. 314, Canberra, 2008, p. 159.

Page 25: '... "pussycats with guts".'

> Judith Brooks, in a letter to *The Australian*, 12 February 2001, p. 12.

Chapter 3

Page 27: 'Managers are necessary; leaders are essential.'

> Sir William Slim, Leadership in management, *Australian Army Journal*, November, No. 102, 1957, p. 7.

Page 27: 'Warfare today is changing faster ...'

> William Lind & Gregory Thiele, *4th Generation Warfare Handbook*, Castalia House, Kouvola, Finland, 2015, p. 1.

Page 28: 'When former Lieutenant Colonel Colin Toll took over as the general manager of the Mount Blue Cow ski resort ...'

> As a Duntroon classmate of Colin's and a keen skier, I spent some time at the resort as his guest during his tenure, and observed how things progressively improved. However, Colin's generosity is unconnected with my evaluation of how his strategy and processes led to business success.

Page 30: '... the perspectives of currently serving junior officers, sergeants and corporals whom I consulted as part of a recent study of Army leadership.'

> Nicholas Jans, What to do and how to think if you want to lead, *Australian Army Journal*, Spring 2016, 13(2), pp. 47–65.

Page 30: 'These junior leaders had observed ...'

> For a scholarly examination of military leadership, see, for example: Donald J. Campbell, Sean T. Hannah & Michael D. Matthews, Leadership in military and other dangerous contexts: Introduction to the special topic issue, *Military Psychology*, April 2010 (online edition); N.A. Jans with David Schmidtchen, *The Real C-Cubed: Culture, careers and climate and how they affect*

military capability, Canberra Papers on Strategy and Defence, No. 143, Strategic & Defence Studies Centre, Australian National University, Canberra, 2002; Nicholas Jans, Shared leadership and the strategic corporal metaphor: Some considerations, in David W. Lovell & Deane-Peter Baker (eds.), *The Strategic Corporal Revisited: Challenges facing combatants in 21st-century warfare*, UCT Press, Cape Town, 2017, pp. 19–31; Thomas Kolditz, *In Extremis Leadership: Leading as if your life depended on it*, Jossey-Bass, San Francisco, CA, 2007; and Eitan Shamir, *Transforming Command: The pursuit of Mission Command in the US, British, and Israeli Armies*, Stanford Security Studies, Stanford University Press, Stanford, CA, 2011.

Page 32: 'Inauthenticity in a leader . . .'

For a seminal treatment of authentic leadership, see Fred O. Walumbwa, Bruce J. Avolio, William L. Gardner, Tara S. Wernsing & Suzanne J. Peterson, Authentic leadership: Development and validation of the theory-based measure, *Journal of Management*, 2008, 34(1), pp. 89–126. For authentic leadership in the military, see Sean T. Hannah, Bruce J. Avolio & Fred O. Walumbwa, Relationships between authentic leadership, moral courage and ethical and pro-social behaviors, *Business Ethics Quarterly*, 2011, 21(4), pp. 555–78.

Page 35: 'Those supported by such teams are thus better able to find the time and mental capacity . . .'

In certain types of chaotic situations, command effectiveness can be enhanced by developing familiarity, intuition and 'commonsense' rules (known as 'heuristics') that come from experience. Such training can also enhance quick reactions in complex situations. But, over-use of intuition and rules may seriously mislead decision-making, causing the decision-maker to proceed blithely but inappropriately. See: Francesca Gino & Don A. Moore, Effect of task difficulty on use of advice, *Journal of Behavioural Decision Making*, 2007, 20, pp. 21–35; and Daniel Kahneman & Gary Klein, Conditions for intuitive expertise: A failure to disagree, *American Psychologist*, 2009, 64, pp. 515–52.

Page 36: 'Military leadership in action'

Nicholas Jans, Shared leadership and the strategic corporal metaphor: Some considerations, in David W. Lovell & Deane-Peter Baker (eds), *The Strategic Corporal Revisited: Challenges facing combatants in 21st-century warfare*, op. cit.

Page 36: 'In short, the *leader-as-catalyst*: overseeing and managing the total process . . .'

Sean T. Hannah, John T. Eggers & Peter L. Jennings, Complex adaptive leadership: Defining what constitutes effective leadership for complex organizational contexts, in G. B. Graen & J. A. Graen (eds.), *The Knowledge-Driven Corporation—Complex creative destruction*, Information Age Publishing Inc., Charlotte, NC, 2008, pp. 79–124; Katherine J. Klein, Jonathan C. Ziegert, Andrew P. Knight & Yan Xiao, Dynamic delegation: Shared, hierarchical, and deindividualized leadership in extreme action teams, *Administrative Science Quarterly*, 2006, 51, pp. 590–621; Douglas R. Lindsay, David V. Day & Stanley Halpin, Shared leadership in the military: Reality, possibility, or pipe dream?, *Military Psychology*, 2011, 23(5), pp. 528–49; and Alex J. Ramthun & Gina S. Matkin, Leading dangerously: A case study of military teams and shared leadership in dangerous environments, *Journal of Leadership & Organisational Studies*, 2014, 21, pp. 244–56.

Page 38: 'This adaptable operational leadership process has many advantages.'

David Schmidtchen, *The Rise of the Strategic Private: Technology, control and change in a network-enabled military*, Land Warfare Studies Centre, Duntroon, ACT, 2006.

Chapter 4

Page 41: 'The day after graduation . . .'

David Gillett, personal communication, March 2001.

Page 41: 'I'm an Australian soldier who is an expert in close combat . . .'

www.army.gov.au/our-people/our-contract-with-australia

Page 42: 'Windsor wrote to Maloney . . .'

Gerard Windsor, *All Day Long the Noise of Battle: An Australian attack in Vietnam*, Pier 9, Sydney, 2011, pp. 13–14.

Page 43: 'Such an ethos has moral as well as practical roots . . .'

See Paddy Griffith, Fighting spirit: leadership and morale on the 'empty battlefield' of the future, in Michael Evans & Alan Ryan (eds), *The Human Face of Warfare: Killing, fear and chaos in battle*, Allen & Unwin, Sydney, 2000, pp. 109–22; Michael Ignatieff, *The Warrior's Honor: Ethnic war and the modern conscience*, Chatto & Windus, London, 1998; and Nicholas Jans, Comparative perspectives: Australia, in Charles C. Moskos & Frank R. Wood (eds), *The Military—More than just a job?*, Pergamon-Brasseys, Elmsford Park, NY, 1988, pp. 211–26.

Page 44: '. . . and consistent with a broader and more systematic study of national service officers of that period . . .'

Warwick Graco & Greg Todd (The Scheyville Association), *A Study of the Effects of Officer Training on a Sample of National*

Servicemen, May 2015 (unpublished) (based on a sample of 225 former national service officers).

Page 48: 'Because this ethos is part of one's self-definition . . .'

See, for example: Marilynn B. Brewer & Wendi Gardner, Who is this 'we'? Levels of collective identity and self representations, *Journal of Personality and Social Psychology*, 1996, 71(1), pp. 83–93; L. Guillén, M. Mayo & K. Korotov, Is leadership a part of me? A leader identity approach to understanding the motivation to lead, *The Leadership Quarterly*, 2015, 26(5), pp. 802–20; Douglas T. Hall, A theoretical model of career sub identity development in organizational settings, *Organizational Behavior and Human Performance*, 1971, 6, pp. 5–76; Sean T. Hannah, Robert L. Woolfolk & Robert G. Lord, Leader self-structure: A framework for positive leadership, *Journal of Organizational Behavior*, 2009, 30, pp. 269–90; Daan van Knippenberg & Michael A. Hogg, A social identity model of leadership effectiveness in organizations, *Research in Organizational Behavior*, 2003, 25, pp. 243–95; and Robert G. Lord & Rosalie J. Hall, Identity, deep structure and the development of leadership skill, *The Leadership Quarterly*, 2005, 16, pp. 591–615.

Page 49: '. . . naval engineer Captain Rachel Durbin . . .'

Navy News, May 5 2016, p. 9.

Page 50: '. . . a report from senior members of a combat signals regiment on the benefits of giving junior NCOs greater opportunities for leadership . . .'

Centre for Army Lessons, Document ID: OBS000034583.

Page 50: 'Its records also provide evidence of the enhanced confidence of Australian soldiers . . .'

Centre for Army Lessons, Document ID: OBS000000427.

Page 53: '... "servant leadership".'

The concept was introduced in an essay by Robert K. Greenleaf (*Servant Leadership: A journey into the nature of legitimate power and greatness*, Paulist Press, Mahwah, NJ, 1977). The concept lay dormant for many years, before being picked up by scholars, the most notable being Professor Robert C. Liden (see, for example: Robert C. Liden, Sandy J. Wayne, Hao Zhao & David Henderson, Servant leadership: Development of a multidimensional measure and multilevel assessment, *Leadership Quarterly*, 2008, 19(2), pp. 161–77; Robert C. Liden, Sandy J. Wayne, Chenwei Liao & Jeremy D. Meuser, Servant leadership and serving culture: Influence on individual and unit performance, *Academy of Management Journal*, 2014, 57(5), pp. 1434–52); and Julia E. Hoch, William H. Bommer, James H. Dulebohn, & Dongyuan Wu, Do ethical, authentic, and servant leadership explain variance above and beyond transformational leadership? A meta-analysis, *Journal of Management*, 2016, 44(2), pp. 501–29. Australian studies include Sen Sendjaya & James Sarros, Servant leadership: Its origins, development and application in organizations, *Journal of Leadership and Organizational Studies*, 2002, 9(2), pp. 57–64; A.A. Pekerti & S. Sendjaya, Exploring servant leadership across cultures: A comparative study in Australia and Indonesia, *The International Journal of Human Resource Management*, 2010, 21(5), pp. 754–80; and Suzanne Seto & James C. Sarros, Servant leadership influence on trust and quality relationships in organizational settings, *International Leadership Journal*, 2016, 8(3), pp. 23–33. The component items on the servant leadership scale used in most of these studies convey its essence, for example: 'Managers and employees at our store put others' best interests ahead of their own' and 'My supervisor makes me feel like I work with him/her, not for him/her'.

Chapter 5

Page 57: 'The standard you walk by is the standard you accept . . .'

As asserted by Lieutenant General David Morrison, AO, in his video address to the Army (available at: www.youtube.com/watch?v=QaqpoeVgr8U).

Page 57: 'Leadership is not about extolling the "special stuff" that sets some apart from others . . .'

S. Alexander Haslam, Stephen D. Reicher & Michael J. Platow, *The New Psychology of Leadership*, op. cit.

Page 58: 'A recent news story provides a new angle on the public perception of military leadership.'

ABC News, 17 February 2016, Highly decorated former Army officer suspected of being senior Bandidos bikie club leader
www.abc.net.au/news/2016-02-17/decorated-former-army-officer-suspected-of-joining-bikie-gang/7175682

Page 59: 'These dozen behaviours broadly encompass what is now recognised as "best practice".'

As noted in the notes on Chapter 1, the 3Rs are very similar to the four dimensions of transformational leadership, a style that is consistently associated with strong commitment and high performance. The table opposite summarises the parallels between the 3Rs model and the transformational dimensions and the quasi-transformational element of transactional leadership that are the core components of full-range leadership. The dimensions of the Human Synergistics model, which is the preferred model for the Navy, are also included.

The 3Rs model compared to two mainstream and widely-used leadership models.

Leadership function: 3Rs		Labels		Relevant activities by the leader	Typical effects on trust	
		Full-range leadership model	Human Synergistics model		Affective (heart)	Cognition (head)
Represent	Lead by example	Idealised influence	Self-actualising	Act in ways that inspire emulation	++	+++
	Give direction and meaning	Inspirational motivation	Achievement	Establish a purpose that focuses and energises	++	+
Relate	Treat members as valued colleagues	Intellectual stimulation	Humanistic-Encouraging	Engage and hence build follower contribution, self-esteem and agency	++	++
	Develop individual and group identity	Individualised consideration	Affiliative	Build social bonds that further enhance self-esteem, confidence and group identity	+	+++
Run the team	Use team activities to build skills and work engagement	Contingency-reward	[Not covered]	Establish a system of formal and informal rules of conduct that, directly and indirectly, continuously remind members of appropriate standards	+++	++
	Encourage open-mindedness and a spirit of continuous improvement	Intellectual stimulation	Humanistic-Encouraging	Engage and hence build follower contribution, self-esteem and agency	++	++

Page 65: 'The performance effects of such an approach are tellingly illustrated in a recent leadership experiment conducted in the Israel Defense Force . . .'

Taly Dvir, Dov Eden, Bruce J. Avolio & Boas Shamir, Impact of transformational leadership on follower development and performance: A field experiment, *Academy of Management Journal*, 2002, 45(4), pp. 735–44. Although it could be argued that the effects of the training received by the platoon commanders could be partly due to a 'Hawthorn effect', in terms of the positive effects of being singled out for special training, there are enough other studies, in civilian as well as military settings, that confirm the primary interpretation of the IDF study. See, for example: Bernard M. Bass, Bruce J. Avolio, Dong I. Jung & Yair Berson, Predicting unit performance by assessing transformational and transactional leadership, op. cit.; Michael E. Brown & Linda K. Treviño, Socialized charismatic leadership, values congruence, and deviance in work groups, *Journal of Applied Psychology*, 2006, 91(4), pp. 954–62; Cam Caldwell, Linda A. Hayes, Do Tien Long, Leadership, trustworthiness, and ethical stewardship, *Journal of Business Ethics*, 2010, 96(4), pp. 497–512; Nicole A. Gillespie & Leon Mann, Transformational leadership and shared values: The building blocks of trust, *Journal of Managerial Psychology*, 2004, 19(6), pp. 588–607; Sean T. Hannah, Bruce J. Avolio & Fred O. Walumbwa, Relationships between authentic leadership, moral courage, and ethical and pro-social behaviors, op. cit.; John M. Schaubroeck, Sean T. Hannah, Bruce J. Avolio, Steve W. J. Kozlowski, Robert G. Lord, Linda K. Treviño, Nikolas Dimotakis & Ann C. Peng, Embedding ethical leadership within and across organizational levels, *Academy of Management Journal*, 2012, 55(5), pp. 1053–78; David Schmidtchen & Alastair Warren, *The Effects of Ethical Leadership on Workforce Behaviour and Performance in the Australian Public Service*, Working Paper, May 2014; and Fred O. Walumbwa, Bruce J. Avolio, William L. Gardner, Tara S. Wernsing & Suzanne J. Peterson, Authentic leadership: Development and validation of a theory-based measure, op. cit.

Page 66: '. . . the application of neuroscience . . .'

See, for example: C. Sue Carter, Oxytocin pathways and the evolution of human behavior, *Annual Review of Psychology*, 2014, 65, pp. 17–39; Pascal Molenberghs, Guy Prochilo, Niklas K. Steffens, Hannes Zacher & S. Alexander Haslam, The neuroscience of inspirational leadership: The importance of collective-oriented language and shared group membership, *Journal of Management*, 2017, 43(7), pp. 2168–94; Russell Cropanzano & William J. Becker, The promise and peril of organizational neuroscience: Today and tomorrow, *Journal of Management Inquiry*, 2013, 22(3), pp. 306–10; Ruth Feldman, Oxytocin and social affiliation in humans, *Hormones and Behavior*, 2012, 61(3), pp. 380–91; and Moïra Mikolajczak, James J. Gross, Anthony Lane, Olivier Corneille, Philippe de Timary & Olivier Luminet, Oxytocin makes people trusting, not gullible, *Psychological Science*, 2010, 21(8), pp. 1072–4.

Page 66: '. . . this double reinforcement effect often occurs within leaders themselves . . .'

Paul J. Zak, The neuroscience of trust: Management behaviors that foster employee engagement, *Harvard Business Review*, 2017, January–February, pp. 84–90.

Chapter 6

Page 69: 'The secret of his popularity lay in the fact that he possessed that rare and indefinable quality . . .'

Rolfe Hartley, *Lessons in Leadership: The life of Sir John Monash GCMG, KCB, VD*, Engineers Australia Sydney Division CELM Presentation, March 2013, p. 10.

Page 69: 'The right words can have a galvanising effect . . .'

Stephen Denning, *The Secret Language of Leadership: How leaders inspire action through narrative*, John Wiley & Sons, San Francisco, CA, 2007, p. 23.

Page 79: '. . . actions by which Salter embedded high standards in the unit and its members.'

Renowned military historian, John Keegan, writes of the importance of soldiers' honour and reputation in his book, *A History of Warfare*, Random House, New York, NY, 1993, p. 48.

Page 81: 'And for at least one afternoon each week, I would practise "management by walking about", as Peters and Waterman had called it.'

Tom Peters & Robert H. Waterman, *In Search of Excellence*, HarperBusiness Essentials, New York, NY, 1982, p. 289.

Chapter 7

Page 87: 'If you asked the diggers about their commanders . . .'

Chris Masters, quoting Lieutenant Ashley Judd, in *Uncommon Soldier*, op. cit., p. 69.

Page 87: 'Paradoxically, in this highly masculine environment filled with extreme danger . . .'

Kara A. Arnold, Catherine Loughlin & Megan M. Walsh, Transformational leadership in an extreme context: Examining gender, individual consideration and self-sacrifice, *Leadership & Organization Development Journal*, 2016, 37(6), pp. 774–88. Quotation taken from p. 785.

Page 89: 'The second quotation at the head of this chapter supports this empirically . . .'

Kara A. Arnold, Catherine Loughlin & Megan M. Walsh, Transformational leadership in an extreme context, op. cit.

Page 90: 'Good people management . . . by consistent attention to many comparatively small things that all add up to something big.'

Abraham Carmeli, Batia Ben-Hador, David A. Waldman & Deborah E. Rupp, How leaders cultivate social capital and nurture employee vigor: Implications for job performance, *Journal of Applied Psychology*, 2009, 94(6), pp. 1553–61.

Page 91: 'Its benefits were confirmed by my recent study . . .'

Nicholas Jans, What to do and how to think if you want to lead, op. cit.

Page 94: 'Navy Warrant Officer Artie Lavender's list of "lessons learned" . . .'

Navy News, September 22 2016, p. 3.

Page 96: '. . . as biographer Ross McMullen writes, his soldiers regarded him as being "absolutely straight, and incapable of deviousness: you knew where you stood with Pompey" . . .'

Ross McMullin, *Pompey Elliott*, Scribe, Melbourne, 2010, p. 82.

Chapter 8

Page 103: 'I suspect that throughout history more good has been done . . .'

Hugh Mackay, Crystal balls-up, *The Sydney Morning Herald*, 28 July 2001.

Page 103: 'One of the Australian Army's greatest advantages . . .'

Major General Jim Molan, personal communication, September 2017.

Page 109: '. . . your leadership style should reflect both current reality and future situations that might be just around the corner . . .'

Bernard M. Bass & Ronald E. Riggio, *Transformational Leadership*, 2nd edn, Lawrence Erlbaum Associates, Inc. New York, NY, 2006.

Chapter 9

Page 119: 'The more I practise, the luckier I get.'

www.shipsticks.com/blog/greatest-golf-quotes-of-all-time/

Page 121: 'Sow early and plant deeply and widely'

For a detailed examination of the principles of leadership development, see David V. Day, The nature of leadership development, in David V. Day & John Antonakis (eds), *The Nature of Leadership*, 2nd edn, Sage, Thousand Oaks, CA, 2012, pp. 108–40.

Page 122: '. . . Australian Defence Force Academy . . .'

In Chapter 3 of his *Uncommon Soldier*, op. cit., Chris Masters describes life at the ADFA and the Royal Military College, Duntroon, with a number of comments from their graduates.

Page 123: 'Given that 83 per cent of Australia's Army officers are men . . .'

Australian Regular Army Workforce Pocket Brief, 1 October 2017.

Page 125: 'Identity'

See the various references on this topic in the notes to Chapter 4.

Pages 128: 'Learning orientation'

David D. Day, The nature of leadership development, op. cit., pp. 115–16; D. Scott DeRue, Susan J. Ashford & Christopher G. Myers, Learning agility: In search of conceptual clarity and theoretical grounding, *Industrial and Organizational Psychology*, 2012, 5, pp. 258–79; and Raymond A. Noe, Alena D.M. Clarke & Howard J. Klein, Learning in the twenty-first century workplace, *Annual Review of Organizational Psychology and Organizational Behavior*, 2014, 1, pp. 245–75.

Pages 130: 'The vital ingredients'

David E. Berlew & Douglas T. Hall, The socialization of managers: Effects of expectations on performance, *Administrative Science Quarterly*, 1966, 11(2), pp. 207–23; Douglas T. Hall, *Careers in Organisations*, Goodyear, Pacific Palisades, CA, 1976; N.A. Jans, Organisational commitment, career factors and career/life stage, *Journal of Organizational Behaviour*, 1989, 10(3), pp. 247–66; and Jenny M. Hoobler, Grace Lemmon & Sandy J. Wayne, Women's managerial aspirations: An organizational development perspective, *Journal of Management*, 2014, 40(3), pp. 703–30.

Chapter 10

Page 135: 'How well you lead, how sharp your own personal discipline . . .'

Australian Army, Junior Leadership on the Battlefield, Australian Army Pamphlet 7610-66-135-0078, 1990, p. 6-1.

Page 135: 'Peter Thomson . . .'

https://en.wikipedia.org/wiki/Peter_Thomson_(golfer)

Page 136: '... a world in which ... leaders and followers alike "must perform at their best on their very worst day".'

My thanks to my colleague, Lieutenant Colonel Adam Gower, for this expression.

Page 139: '... *leading from the shadows* ...'

Nicholas Jans, Social and political acumen: A vital but neglected professional skill set, *Australian Defence Force Journal*, July/ August 2017, pp. 83–9 (www.defence.gov.au/adc/adfj/). See also Jean Hartley, John Alford, Owen Hughes & Sophie Yates, *Leading with Political Astuteness: A study of public managers in Australia, New Zealand and the United Kingdom*, ANZSOG and CM, Melbourne, 2013; and Gerald R. Ferris, Darren C. Treadway, Robert W. Kolodinsky, Wayne A. Hochwarter, Charles J. Kacmar, Ceasar Douglas & Dwight D. Frink, Development and validation of the political skill inventory, *Journal of Management*, 2005, 31, pp. 126–52.

Page 139 : '... *leading from the top.*'

Nicholas Jans, with Stephen Mugford, Jamie Cullens & Judy Frazer-Jans, *The Chiefs: A study of strategic leadership*, Australian Defence College, Canberra, 2013 (www.defence.gov.au/adc/ publications/chiefs/thechiefs.pdf).

Appendix 1

Page 145: 'The Army comprises ... serving part time.'

Department of Defence Annual Report 2016–17, October 2017, Table 7.2 (p. 84) and Table 7.5 (p. 86) (http://www.defence.gov.au/ annualreports/16-17/Downloads/DAR_2016-17_Complete.pdf).

Index

After Action Review (AAR) 115–16
agency 31, 64, 67, 116
  defined 155
Alexander, Gordon 82
Allan, Gary 114–15
Alpha, Lieutenant Commander 49
Appleton, Brigadier Chris 79
Australian Army
  ranks 147
  structure 145–6
Australian Defence Force 2011–12
    investigations into sexual
    harassment 7
Australian Defence Force Academy,
    ACT 122
Australian national leadership
    studies
  Australian Cultural Imprints
    Studies 23

Melbourne University Centre for
    Workplace Leadership 5

Bandidos motor cycle gang,
    leadership of 58, 66–7
Bravo, Group Captain 49–50
Brown, Chris 73
Bryon, Ernie 43–4, 100, 132–3

Calonge, Generoso 83
Cantwell, Major General John 3–5,
    11, 18, 79
Cater, Nick 20
Centre for Army Lessons,
    Puckapunyal, VIC 50
Chapman, Colin 43, 47
Charlie, Lieutenant Colonel 54
Chiefs, The 140
Clement, Jim 92, 108

commanding officer, defined 155
Crawford, Colonel Mike vii, 133
Crowe, Russell 101–2

Delta, Brigadier 54–5
Durbin, Captain Rachel 49

Earle, Terry 43, 45, 73
Echo, Major 70–1, 79, 84, 112
Elliott, Bruce 107–8
Elliott, Major General Harold
    ('Pompey') 96

FFANF principles 96
Fischer, Tim 43, 46
followership, defined 15, 155
Foxtrot, Warrant Officer 93

Gabriel, Brigadier Shane 24
Gale, Neville 130–1
George, Major Bob 114
Gillett, David 41
Gladiator 101
Golf, Major 93–4
Gowans, Patrick 78, 95, 98, 112
Graham, Peter 43, 51–2, 82, 83,
    111–12, 114, 132, 134

Hawkins, Jon 14
Hayward, Lieutenant Colonel
    Duncan 100, 107
Henry V 117–18
Hewitt, Peter 48
Hiley, The Honourable Justice
    Graham 73
Hirst, John 19–20

Hotel, Warrant Officer 94–5
Howard, Major General Brian
    ('Hori') 93
Howes, Peter 75
Hunter, Governor John 20

India, Corporal 96
Israel Defense Force 65–6

Jackson, Brigadier Wayne 80–1
Juliet, Lieutenant 97

Keating, Major General Mike 77
Kendall, Wayne 100
Kennett, Jeff 33–4, 43, 46
Kerntke, Captain Peter 73–4
Kilo, Wing Commander 97–8
King, Amanda 95, 112
King, Lieutenant Colonel Mick 75,
    93, 104–5

Lavender, Warrant Officer Artie 94
leaders, defined 15, 156
leadership
    analogy to Tolstoy's observation on
        families in *Anna Karenina* 10
    Australian military distinctiveness
        2–3
    authoritative vs. authoritarian 6,
        155
    defined 15, 156
    development of 120–134
        character and values 127
        identity 125
        learning orientation 128

vital ingredients in
  autonomy 131–2
  challenge 130–1
  feedback and support 132–4
ethos 41, 156
human evolution, and 18
identity leadership 19
inauthenticity 32–3
leader-as-catalyst 36, 38, 156
management, in contrast to 33, 157
mission-team-me priorities 51
neuroscience, insights from 66
process of building trust and
  exercising influence 17–18,
  65–6
servant leadership 53, 118, 158
stereotypes of military leadership
  24–5
strategic leadership 140
values-based leadership 16–17
national evolution, and 19
perspectives of currently serving
  junior personnel 30–2
Lima, Warrant Officer 98–9
Linwood, Russell 54, 74, 99, 116
Longhurst, John 99

McCallum, Professor John 43, 47,
  76, 117, 129–30
McMullen, Ross 96
Maloney, Mark 42, 55
Marysville xv, 3, 11, 18, 59, 79
  Marysville Community Golf &
    Bowls Club xvi, 79–80
Master and Commander 101
Masters, Chris 89, 91

Mike, Flight Lieutenant 113
military appreciation process 72,
  150–1, 157
military leadership culture
  civilian misperceptions of 7
  distinctive features of 8
  leadership ethos of 41, 156
  'taking the principles of war and
    applying them to peace' 25
mission command 111, 151–2, 157
Molan, Major General Jim 34–5,
  103
Monash, General Sir John 13, 64, 69
morale, defined 157
Morrison, Lieutenant General David
  xiii–xiv, 9, 57, 136
Morgan, Peter 133
Mount Blue Cow ski resort 28–30,
  38–9
Mueller, Lieutenant General Des 93

networked hierarchy 36–8, 157
Newman, Miles 109
Noble, Brigadier Roger 48, 151
non-commissioned officer, defined
  157

officer, defined 157
Officer Cadet School, Portsea, VIC
  83
Officer Training Unit, Scheyville,
  NSW 43

Pagel, Professor Mark 18
Pierce, David 92, 96
Player, Gary 142

Ramsay, Don 108, 131–2
Reynolds, Major Bill 110
Rhoden, Dr Clare 22
Royal Military College, Duntroon,
    ACT 122–3

Salter, Lieutenant Colonel John 78
Schlumberger Oilfield Exploration
    120
Scott, Major Bruce 78
Scott, Mark 53
Senior, Rob 73
Slater, Bob 74
SMEAC communication protocol
    81–4, 152–3, 158
social and political acumen 139–40

Thatcher, Warren 99–100
Thomson, Peter 136, 142
Three Block War 24, 158
Toll, Colin 28, 30, 35, 39, 105
trust, defined 158
Turnbull, Noel xvii, 88, 101

values, defined 158

Whitaker, Dick 92
Whitelaw, Peter 128–9
Williams, Ray 127
Windsor, Gerard 42, 55

Yeo, Milly 78, 98